More

COURT

JESTERS

More Court Jesters

Back to the Bar
for More of the Funniest Stories
from Canada's Courts

Peter V. MacDonald, Q.C.

Illustrations by David Brown

METHUEN
Toronto   New York   London   Sydney   Auckland

For Catherine,
Michael, Shaun
and Mary

Canadian Cataloguing in Publication Data

MacDonald, Peter V. (Peter Vincent), 1934-
  More court jesters

ISBN 0-458-81170-X

1. Courts – Canada – Anecdotes, facetiae,
satire, etc.   2. Law – Canada – Anecdotes,
facetiae, satire, etc.   I. Title.

K184.7CM32 1987   347.71′01′0207   C87-093983-1

Printed and bound in the United States
1 2 3 4 5   87   92 91 90 89 88

Contents

Acknowledgments

With the exception of my children, Michael, Shaun, and Mary, no one will ever know what my dear, patient, loyal, loving wife Catherine has endured. She's survived two books! Do you know what that *means*? It means she's durable, tough, maybe even indestructible, because she's read hundreds of humorous stories sent to me by hundreds of people who are trying desperately to break into big-time showbiz and, what's more, she's had to listen to me tell many of these stories over and over again, and not once has she cracked! Oh, she's come close a few times, but she's never quite slipped over that line, you know what I mean? Catherine deserves a medal. Make that two.

Michael, Shaun, and Mary rate a medal each – mainly for listening to the stories and refraining at all times from making disparaging remarks about them. Also, they were very good about chatting up the book(s) with potential purchasers. Come to think of it, so was my niece, Allison Rankine, who frequently went so far as to try out some of my material on people who came to visit her and couldn't leave without being rude. Now that's what I call loyalty. Allison gets a medal and three subway tokens.

Many thanks to my secretaries, Karen Glasser, Charlotte Valles, and Sheila Stephenson, all of whom allowed me to try out stories on them and never once told me to get lost. The same goes for Frank Schuler, Sandra Roach, Liz Graham, and Charleen Castellan. Thanks, too, to Barb Schuler, Shannon Beaudin, and my daughter Mary for assisting Karen Glasser with typing the manuscript.

I also wish to thank my former colleague, William French, the esteemed literary editor of *The Globe and Mail*, for the assistance and encouragement he gave me in getting started in this line of work. If it hadn't been for Bill, *Court Jesters* and *More Court Jesters* might still be nothing more than fond dreams.

Thanks also go to the Osgoode Hall Law School Alumni Association, the Nova Scotia Barristers' Society, and the Law Society of Newfoundland for various kindnesses extended to me in my efforts to track down humorous legal stories. In that connection, a crackerjack secretary in Edmonton, Corinne Skura, should also take a bow.

Finally, thanks to the nearly five hundred Canadians who bombarded me with humorous anecdotes and valuable leads for this book. You were indispensable.

Hanover, Ontario
April 1987

Foreword

by

Edward L. Greenspan, Q.C.

The law is a deeply, deadly, serious business but it is an error to suppose that our law has no sense of humour. The scope of this book is indicated by its title – the lighter side of the law, as it is exhibited from time to time in the witty remarks, repartées, and bon mots of the bench and bar of Canada. The author scans the courtroom, the judges' chambers, the lawyers' offices, and all due processes of law looking for, finding, and revealing the humour that is a true and enduring part of law.

Humour is the healthy refusal to take oneself, one's institutions, one's customs, one's way of life, too seriously. Some may suggest that this book has no message, that it preaches no doctrine, and that it is written solely to provoke laughter. I think there is a serious point to this very humorous book. These pages prove that, fortunately for us all, even while engaged in the lofty endeavour of the pursuit of justice through the administration of law, people still can take the time to laugh at themselves. This book is full of whimsical moments – the interludes that lighten just a little the grim and sorrowful world of the courtroom. Even the stark reality of the legal system is packed with perplexities, inconsistencies, incongruities, and absurdities – the stuff of which laughter is made.

For many, it will be comforting to learn from the pages of this book that judges are people who remain human even after assuming their judicial duties. Like all the rest of mankind they may be affected from time to time by pride and passion, by pettiness and bruised feelings, by improper understanding, or by excessive zeal. But what we learn above all else from this book is that judges are not always dull and solemn. They can be funny, both in and out of court.

The chapter on the "Polish Prince" will make all Canadians feel confident that the law is well served by judges like Mr. Justice Wachowich of the Queen's Bench of Alberta. Give me any judge who says "the best medicine is a good belly laugh." Chief Justice Gregory Evans's witty reply to a questionnaire will help you to understand why he enjoys such an incredible reputation as a Supreme Court judge.

Beset by weighty decisions that have to be made and important issues that have to be resolved, it is refreshing to see that judges realize that laughter is the safety valve which prevents blowing one's top al-together. This collection of stories and anecdotes illustrates the funny side of the street.

As Mr. MacDonald appreciates so well, truth is stranger than fiction. "The Case of the Blue Tick Hound" and "The Martians Are Coming! The Martians Are Coming!" remind us that some of the best entertainment in town goes on in the courtrooms of our land.

Many writers have analyzed the question of what it takes to become an accomplished lawyer. Some argue that it is necessary to have a knowledge of the law, of history, of science, of philosophy, of the modes of business. Others argue that it is necessary to be a well-read person of large understanding. Some say a good lawyer must be a fine orator, must have sympathy, tact, and courtesy and must know people and their ways. All agree that a lawyer must be courageous, forthright, of incorruptible integrity, and have a high sense of honour. Sadly, the literature on this subject is almost devoid of any reference to humour. To me, a good sense of humour is an essential part of the makeup of a lawyer. Humour breaks courtroom tension and preserves sanity. It puts things into perspective.

While recognizing their faults, I have a good opinion of lawyers. I enjoy working with them, fighting with them, and laughing with them. Believe it or not, some lawyers are very funny people. I have never met a more engaging person than The Honourable Judge David Humphrey. Before his recent appointment to the bench, his fantastic sense of humour would have to be listed among the numerous qualities that made him one of the greatest criminal lawyers in Canadian history.

Peter MacDonald has recorded some wonderful examples of lawyers' humour. Walton Cook's remark at the opening of a session of the Supreme Court of Nova Scotia is as funny a line as was ever said anywhere in Canada.

In *Court Jesters*, the author collected humorous incidents that had happened in courts from Newfoundland to British Columbia. In this book, he proves that he only scratched the surface of legal humour in Canada in his first book.

In another place, I have stated that there is no better symbol of our judicial system than the scales of justice, for it is these scales that represent impartiality and total objectivity. Mr. MacDonald shows us that laughter, in and out of court, is the only true antidote, the only tonic to the high solemnity regularly observed in the courtrooms of our great land.

Introduction

My cup runneth over. I'm a lucky fellow, indeed.

People keep sending me stories that make me laugh – stories about funny things that are said in and around our courts. I pass these yarns on to others, and that causes a goodly number of them to laugh, too. It also frequently reminds them of humorous legal anecdotes that have been hibernating in their heads for lengthy periods, and many of these folks are kind enough to convey such material to me. Then there I am, laughing again – and again and again. It's a vicious – make that hilarious – circle. My day often starts with a batch of funny mail. Since laughter makes one feel good all over, this is a hell of a nice way to launch a day. You might say I've been spoiled. If you did, you'd be right.

At least I share the booty. My first bundle of legal laughs appeared in 1985 in a jolly volume entitled *Court Jesters*. It's still doing nicely, thank you, and now its kid brother, *More Court Jesters*, is clamouring for your attention. If you have half as much fun reading it as I had researching and writing it, you'll be pleased that you made its acquaintance.

The response to the first book has been marvellous. I knew that lawyers, judges, and others connected with the law would enjoy such a production, but I didn't expect the general public to "dig" it as much as they did. Many people have told me that, since reading *Court Jesters*, they've revised their opinion of us "legal types." They said they now realized that a fair number of lawyers and judges were, well, human. Previously, they'd had most of us pegged as pompous, arrogant bastards. A Toronto man phoned me to say that he'd been so despondent from years of never-ending litigation that he'd contemplated committing suicide – until he read *Court Jesters*. "I never laughed so hard in my life," he said, "and it wasn't long before I had my perspective back." Whew!

It shouldn't be surprising that humorous legal stories have universal appeal. After all, people crave laughter – if they don't get some every now and then they could slip their trolleys – and the courts have always been a fertile source of amusement. They're certainly not *meant* to be, but every now and then, for a moment or so, they *become* that way. Why? It's all tied in with tension – sometimes unbearable tension. When adversaries and their witnesses clash in the high-voltage setting of a court of law – a setting that's foreign and scary to most of them – weird and wonderful words often tumble out of their mouths. Yes, sir, the courtroom is the best free show in town.

A quick example. In a courtroom in Port Hawkesbury, Nova Scotia, not long ago, a woman went on and on about what a "devil" her husband was. "The devil's drunk half the time, he's abusive to me, he gambles the rent at the racetrack," she told Judge Lew Matheson. "I tell you, Your Honour, he's a devil!"

"Well, we'll just cut off the devil's tail," Judge Matheson said.

"Oh, I've already done that," the woman remarked, "but that just made him worse than before!"

In a review of *Court Jesters*, Provincial Court Judge Dennis E. Fenwick of Regina notes: "Humour is the tonic which makes the practice of law more tolerable, the elixir which removes the frustration of being damned and praised, hated and loved, for equally inappropriate reasons. Humour is a welcome break from the electric excitement of hearing your 7,000th breathalyzer case." Right on, Your Honour!

There's all kinds of medical and scientific proof that laughter is beneficial to your health. "A hearty laugh gives a workout to your stomach and chest muscles, heart and lungs," one authority writes. "And though your blood pressure and adrenalin go up during laughter, they drop to a normal level or below afterwards, releasing stress. Laughter *is* the best medicine."

A 105-year-old Toronto woman recently told a reporter that her sense of humour is the secret of her longevity. "If you like a joke and you like to laugh, you'll live a long time," she said. "I see the funny side of everything and I can tell a good joke. That's what's kept me around so long."

Judging from the enthusiastic support I've received from every part of the country, a great many folks are solidly in favour of laughter. Well over three hundred people contributed stories (or tips as to where I could get stories) when I was preparing *Court Jesters*. For this book, close to five hundred obliging souls chipped in. They're listed at the back of the book. I might have missed a few. If I did, I regret it. I'll get you for sure the next time.

I'm flattered that one of Canada's foremost criminal lawyers, Edward L. Greenspan, Q.C., interrupted his extremely busy schedule to read my manuscript and write the Foreword to this book. Eddie is a brilliant, witty fellow – and obviously a person of discriminating taste.

One other matter. In the last couple of years, quite a few people who are also endowed with discriminating taste have seen fit to have me appear in public, with my bare face hanging out, and tell my funniest legal stories to wildly appreciative audiences. If you're interested in following suit, arrangements can be made through **Laura M. Ferrier & Associates Inc., 2510 Yonge St., Toronto, Ontario, M4P 2H7; telephone (416) 440-0463.**

Now let's get on with the show, shall we? And remember, laughing is good for your health.

1

The Martians Are Coming!
The Martians Are Coming!

During the evening of May 30 and the wee hours of May 31, 1985, two men we'll call Jones and Smith drove in a truck through the Ontario counties of Huron and Bruce, stopping frequently for fresh transfusions of grog. It was a night to remember – if only they could. These fellows were plastered.

At about 3:30 A.M., near the village of Formosa, Jones braked and stopped the truck behind a van that was parked on the shoulder of the road. Smith was asleep in the passenger seat.

Jones scrambled out of his vehicle and staggered up to the van. He rapped on the window and woke the sole occupant, a man named Panayote Alafoyannis. Startled, Alafoyannis opened the door slightly and peered into the inky night.

"What are you doing here?" roared the intruder.

Alafoyannis didn't wait to answer. "I locked the door," he later told police. "The man punched the window and yelled, 'Come on outside and I'll kill you!' Then he started rocking the van."

After a while Jones left, got into his truck, and backed it into a ditch. "I saw him and another guy walk to a farm house," Alafoyannis said. "They came back and the other guy got back into the truck. Then the first guy came back to my van again and started hollering, 'Come out and I'll kill you!' "

Alafoyannis had had enough. He honked his horn several times, and a few seconds later two dozen strange-looking little men came running through the darkness, heading for the van.

Jones gulped when he got a good look at the stubby apparitions that milled around him. They were all about five feet tall and wore metal hats with lights on them. Aprons with big pockets covered their legs, and bulky baskets hung from their necks.

"Martians!" Jones screamed as he ran through a thicket of bobbing lights.

A few minutes later, Jones pounded on the door of a farm house, shouting all the while that Martians were in the neighbourhood.

Before the man of the house could make it to the door, Jones lurched over to a nearby station wagon, the key to which was in the ignition. The man arrived at the door just in time to see his wife's car speeding up the laneway. He called the Ontario Provincial Police at Walkerton, about seven miles to the east, and reported what had happened.

OPP constables Kevin Washnuk and John Potts had just driven out of their detachment, at the edge of Walkerton, when they spotted the station wagon that had been reported stolen a few minutes earlier. They did a quick U-turn, caught up with Jones, and stopped him. Jones staggered when he got out of the car.

"Thank God you're here!" he said excitedly. "I was just coming to get you! You won't *believe* what happened! The Martians have landed and you gotta *do* something!"

"Sure, sure," the officers said as they booked Jones for car theft.

"No, guys, I really saw Martians – little wee fellows with lights on their foreheads! They're kicking the shit outta my buddy, and I just had to get here so you'd know what happened and you could go out there and *do* something about it!"

The police officers told Jones he was also charged with impaired driving, and they demanded a sample of his breath. He refused and was slapped with another charge – failing to provide a breath sample.

At about 4:40 A.M. constables Washnuk and Potts found Jones's pickup truck in the ditch. Smith was sprawled across the front seat, still asleep. The officers questioned him, and it was apparent that he'd missed the entire invasion.

A few minutes later the officers saw quite a few lights in a nearby field. They got up close and saw, in Washnuk's words, "two dozen men, all about five feet tall, some on their knees, some squatting, some crouched over." They wore metal hats with lights shining out of the front, Washnuk said, and they wore "slimy, dirty aprons." And they had baskets hanging from their necks.

So Jones was *right*, right? These fellows *really were* Martians, right? Wrong!

They were Japanese-Canadian wormpickers, up from Toronto, pulling in another commercial "catch."

None of them could speak English, so the police weren't able to worm anything out of them. But they got a statement from foreman Panayote Alafoyannis, and when Crown Attorney Brian Farmer learned the whole story he agreed with defence counsel Jim Donnelly that Jones, in his drunken state, honestly believed he was up to his arse in Martians and had to swipe the car to flee to safety. So the theft charge was dropped, and Jones pleaded guilty to impaired driving and failing to provide a breath sample.

And, it is hoped, everyone lived happily ever after.

As Toronto lawyer Walton (Wally) Rose once remarked after a particularly wacky case: "And to think that we get paid for this sort of thing!"

Yes, indeed, lawyers and judges are very fortunate people. Though the matters that command their attention are serious and rarely exciting, it's always possible that something weird and wonderful will pop up to brighten their day. That blessed balm called laughter is always available, just around the corner.

Usually you don't even have to go looking for it. It comes to you – in the form, say, of a witty comment or a colourful witness or a ludicrous situation – and for a while you feel good all over. Maybe this is why so many lawyers are still practising in their eighties, and some in their nineties, while most other folks are packing it in as early as they can.

Some of the things that happen in our courts, and many of the things said therein, are downright daffy. You never know what will come up in the courtroom, "the best free show in town." Some folks don't like this. They want everything to be predictable, which, of course, it can't be. Why, to hear them talk, you'd think our courts had gone to the dogs.

In a way, maybe they're right.

The late Judge James G. Harvie of Barrie, Ontario, had a teeny-weeny chihuahua dog that he carried around in his vest pocket almost everywhere he went – including court. The pooch usually snoozed on a small purple pillow, atop the judge's bench, but sometimes he followed the proceedings with great interest. "He'd be sitting on the bench, looking down at you," said lawyer Edward B. Kendall of nearby Midland. "It was strange."

Many a time, I'm told, lawyers, court officials, and others were treated to the memorable sight of dog and master entering court.

"This court is now in session," the clerk would announce. The door would open and out would walk the chihuahua, followed by Judge Harvie. The dog would head straight for the dais and the judge would place him on the comfy purple pillow.

Legal people agree that Harvie was a good judge, but he and his dog were inseparable. When it came to his pet, the master's motto was: "Don't leave home without it."

Judge Harvie was a stickler for proper courtroom dress and decorum. Pity the lawyer who wore brown shoes or had light-coloured pants on under his gown! He was in for a scathing sermon about the absolute necessity of counsel showing the highest respect for the court.

Ernest Miller, who for many years was a sheriff's officer in Barrie, recalls the time a hapless lawyer endured a tough tongue-lashing on how he was attired. As Judge Harvie preached on, his chihuahua peeked out from under his robes, looked squarely at the lawyer, and nodded in full agreement.

Collingwood lawyer Robert C. Thompson, Q.C., says he'll never forget his first appearance before Judge Harvie. Bob was aware of His Honour's reputation for rigidly adhering to the rules of courtroom etiquette, and in this, his debut, he was determined to do everything perfectly. He bowed and scraped in all the right places.

Then it happened. Judge Harvie asked Thompson to hand him a certain document. Bob bowed low and handed the document up to the judge. Just then the chihuahua jumped out from the judicial robes, sped across the bench and snapped at the lawyer's hand. Thompson saw this at the last split-second and stepped back quickly. "I've never been so startled in my life," he says. "The little bugger almost bit my finger."

Chief Judge G. L. Bladon, of the Territorial Court of the Yukon, tells of a canine caper in his court in Dawson City:

"I was about to embark upon the hearing of a charge of break, enter, and theft. The courtroom at that time was small, stuffy, and overcrowded, being located directly over the liquor store. The accused allegedly had broken into the dog pound and retrieved his own dog. Both the accused and the dog were well-known characters at the time in Dawson City.

"When the clerk called the case, the accused, unrepresented, shuffled to the front of the courtroom with a twinkle in his eye and an Irish Wolfhound by his side.

"In an effort to silence the titters that were breaking out around the courtroom, I said, in the sternest voice I could manage, 'Mr. Watt, get that dog out of here!'

"Came the response: 'But Your Honour, he's a witness!' "

Dean Jobb, a reporter with the Halifax *Chronicle-Herald*, has a story about a dog that *did* testify – sort of.

A Nova Scotia man charged with having a vicious dog sat in court, his dog at his feet, and listened as several witnesses described how the mutt had snapped at them and scared them half to death.

"Is there any evidence you'd like to present?" the judge asked the accused when the others had finished.

"Yes, Your Honour," the accused replied. "I'd like to call my dog to testify."

"What?"

"I'd like to call my dog to testify."

"A dog can't testify."

"Your Honour, I've been here all morning with my dog, waiting for this case to be called and listening to the testimony of the witnesses. All that time, my dog's been sitting here with me. There've been a lot of people milling around and the dog hasn't jumped at anyone. How can they say this is a fierce and vicious dog?"

The judge thought for a moment.

"I agree," he said. "Case dismissed."

Judge Walder G. W. White of the Provincial Court of Alberta has a dandy yarn about the late, legendary Mr. Justice Harold Riley of the Supreme Court of Alberta.

"Mr. Justice Riley was quite a character. He had a large standard-bred poodle that was practically the size of a Great Dane. He and the dog were inseparable, and he took the dog to the courthouse almost every day. The dog's name was Rousseau.

"One day, in Red Deer, Rousseau had come into the court with the judge and was sitting at his feet under the bench, unseen by the audience in court. Mr. Justice Riley dropped a pencil. When he leaned over to pick it up, he fell on the floor with a big bang and disappeared from sight. The noise startled everyone in the courtroom and they looked up, and so did Rousseau. You can picture their surprise when all they could see above the judge's bench was the head of this large dog.

"Mr. Justice Riley pulled himself to his knees and looked up as well. Now there were two heads, at the same level, peering over the bench. The judge looked at the dog, immediately realized the situation, and turned to the audience and said, 'It's okay. He writes all my judgments!' "

Some trials go on for weeks, some even for months. A recent trial in Hamilton, Ontario, lasted a year and a half. Toronto lawyer Garry K.

Braund, Q.C., happened to hear what could well be the shortest trial in history.

An elderly woman was charged with breaking a city anti-noise by-law by playing her radio too loudly at three in the morning. When the clerk of the court had read the charge to the accused, she cupped her left ear and said, "Eh?"

The clerk read the charge again.

"Eh?"

He read the charge a third time.

"Eh?"

For the fourth time, the clerk read out the charge.

"Eh?"

The justice of the peace realized the woman was practically deaf. Now it was *his* turn to say something.

"Case dismissed."

If you like slapstick, Richard N. Clarke, Q.C., of Orillia, Ontario, has a couple of treats for you.

A few years back, Clarke had a trial with a lawyer who shall remain nameless. The lawyer had one of those huge briefcases that would accommodate two dozen bottles of beer, and he placed it on the floor near his seat at the counsel table.

"I'd been giving this fellow a pretty hard time all morning," Clarke confesses, "and when I said something that absolutely incensed him he jumped to his feet, stepped into his briefcase, and fell flat on his keester."

Astounded by what he'd seen, the lawyer's client couldn't help blurting out: "Your Honour, look at my *lawyer*! He's on his *ass!*"

Another time, Clarke and his friend, Crown Attorney John S. Alexander, Q.C., locked horns in a five-day attempted-murder case. As is the custom, the lawyers had been using a lectern throughout the trial. When one of the lawyers rose to ask questions of a witness or to address the judge or the jury, he'd borrow the lectern his opponent was using, place his notes on its slanted surface, and swing into action. Often, as is also the custom, he'd lean on the lectern as he spoke.

The evidence had all been presented, and it was time for the lawyers to make their closing addresses to the jury – first Alexander, then Clarke.

Clarke is shortish, Alexander is about six-foot-three. The lectern they'd been using was just fine for a man of Alexander's height. Not so for Clarke, who'd "spent the whole week leaning up." So, just before the start of the addresses, Clarke got a lectern that was about eight inches shorter than the other one and placed it in front of the jury box. He neglected to tell his opponent about the switch.

When court reconvened, Alexander bowed to the judge, strode over to the lectern, spread his papers on it and began: "Ladies and gentlemen of the jury, there may be no more serious task for a citizen to perform than to serve on a jury . . ." Then he leaned forward on the lectern and tumbled into the jury box, amid hoots of laughter from the jurors.

Mr. Justice George L. Murray of the Supreme Court of British Columbia sent me the transcript of a trial held in Prince George. A Prince George lawyer, William Firman, had picked up several traffic tickets, and he went before Provincial Court Judge George O. Stewart to face the music. This is the tune he heard:

THE CLERK: Number 64, William Firman.
MR. FIRMAN: I'm appearing for myself, Your Honour.
THE COURT: I've found you guilty and you are ordered flogged. What do you want to do, Mr. Firman?
MR. FIRMAN: I want to dispose of this matter.
THE COURT: Very well. I've got nine – eight counts. Do you want to plead guilty or not guilty?
MR. FIRMAN: I do.
THE COURT: You're not getting married?
MR. FIRMAN: No way.
THE COURT: No.
MR. FIRMAN: Not today.
THE COURT: How do you want to plead to these?
MR. FIRMAN: Guilty.
THE COURT: All right. Get the faggots and the gas. Oh, dear me . . . Honestly, this place is unreal. Oh, Lord. It's a fine of five dollars on counts 1 and 2 and a suspended sentence on the rest.
MR. FIRMAN: Two weeks to pay?
THE COURT: Oh, nonsense. You'll spend that much on lunch. Go forth and sin no more, my son.

Chief Judge Harold Gyles of the Provincial Court of Manitoba kindly supplied a transcript of the evidence given by a man charged with obstructing a highway. "The case was tried twenty years ago," Judge Gyles told me, "and there's such a good lesson in here for overzealous policemen that most RCMP recruits who've come along since then have received a copy of this transcript for careful consideration."

After a Mountie had testified, the judge asked the accused, "Is there anything you wish to say?"

"There certainly is, Your Honour."

"All right, take the witness box."

Word for word, here's the man's evidence:

"I was on my way to buy hay for a horse ranch, which I have down on No. 4 Highway. My ranch foreman was in a car proceeding north ahead of me. He didn't know this cut-off to go down to No. 59 on the Perimeter Highway. So I swung around the corner going east, part way toward the underpass. I stopped my car – it was running – and I opened the door and was honking my horn and waving at him to come back.

"You see, our farm is about ten miles past that, where we breed race horses, and we were out to buy hay that afternoon. We were going to Bird's Hill and he went past and didn't know where to turn off, so I turned partially in there and was honking and waving my arms, and he stopped on the overpass when the officer came up behind me.

"Now he came up behind me, and as an officer of the law I don't think he was justified in what he was doing, because first of all he says, 'Pull up ahead there,' which I did, and he grabs a plastic jug out of my car. I am a responsible citizen. I don't use home brew. I have a farm and everything. He pulls the jug out of my car and pours some in his hand and licked at it like a dog (demonstrating), which is true as long as I stand here and hold this Bible.

"What he was looking for, I don't know. He wanted to give me a ticket and he didn't know what to give it for, and that's all it was. And if he knew what I carried in that bottle, he wouldn't have licked the stuff out of that bottle, let me tell you.

"I have breeding mares and I take the urine to the vet all the time, and that's what I use the bottle for, and that is the honest-to-God truth. And he had to give me a ticket for something, because he figured he got to give me a ticket, that's all."

THE COURT: For tasting your sample?

A. I guess it tasted so good, he wanted to know where I lived, to get more . . .

THE COURT: Thank you very much. I am going to acquit you.

Mr. Justice Claude R. Vallerand of the Court of Appeal of Quebec has the rare distinction of having served on three different courts in his native province – the Municipal Court, the Superior Court, and the Court of Appeal. He writes:

"Tradition commands that a new judge be lenient in his first sentence and hence that the first accused brought before him be worthy of mercy, the quality of which, it has been said, is not strained.

"So it was that on my first night in the Municipal Court of Repentigny, Quebec, a trembling little old lady was called forth, charged with having watered her beloved flower beds at some other than the opportune time.

"Trembling little old lady (pleading guilty): *'Cou . . . coup . . . coupable, Son Honneur.'*

"Stern new judge: *'Sentence suspendue.'*

"Trembling little old lady drops to the floor.

"I later learned from the attending officer that her tired legs had given way as she heard 'pendue' and understood that she had been sentenced to hang."

Vancouver lawyer Sidney B. (Slippery Sid) Simons tells a story about the late Judge Nick Mussallem of the Provincial Court of British Columbia. A deaf-mute charged with shoplifting appeared before Judge Mussallem and pleaded guilty to the charge.

The prosecutor told the court the facts of the case. Then defence counsel made a "pitch" on behalf of his client, stressing the fact that it was his first offence. Everything the judge and lawyers said was relayed to the accused by a translator who used sign language.

"All right," Judge Mussallem said to the translator, "don't tell the accused what I'm going to say now. Just wait."

His Honour turned to the accused and proclaimed:

"The sentence of this court upon you is that you be taken from here to the place whence you came and there be kept in close confinement until the fourteenth day of the next month, and upon that date that you be taken to the place of execution and that you be there hanged by the neck until you are dead. *And may the Lord have mercy upon your soul.*"

Then, with a smile of infinite gratification, Judge Mussallem said to counsel, "I've always wanted to say that!" Immediately thereafter, with the translator back in action, His Honour gave the *real* sentence – suspended sentence.

Judge G. Hughes Randall of the Provincial Court of Nova Scotia recalls a case in which an accused man admitted on the stand that on the night in question he was drunk, whereupon a local rummy rose unsteadily from his seat and shouted: "Twenty years!"

Dave Brown, a columnist on the Ottawa *Citizen*, tells a story that's regarded as a classic in Ottawa legal circles. One of his newspaper colleagues, the late Joe Finn, a notorious prankster, wanted to show up a pompous court official who read out the names, addresses, and occupations of prospective jurors.

"This fellow would scream out the names as they were drawn from the drum," Brown recalled recently, "and he'd *always* mispronounce them badly. The same with the other information.

"Joe was going to fix this guy. Somehow he got a hold of a blank disc, filled it out, put it in the drum, and then disappeared. He didn't want to be in court if and when the disc was drawn."

Next day, the disc found its way into the hand of the court official. Written on it were the words: *"Zotique Vrzalkovski, R.R.1, Carp, Pheasant Plucker."*

For the first and only time in his long career, the fellow got all the information absolutely right!

Toronto lawyer Robert B. McGee, Q.C., recalls the time, a few years ago, that a rookie court clerk was handed a piece of paper by Judge William F. Rogers with the instructions, "Mark this as an exhibit."

The nervous young clerk grabbed the judge's right wrist and stamped the back of his hand.

"No, not that one!" Judge Rogers exclaimed. So the clerk grabbed His Honour's other hand and stamped it, too.

The main area of the village of Sherbrooke, Nova Scotia, has been restored to look as it did in the 1850s. Tourists flock there in the summer, admiring the old-style architecture and doing business with merchants and craftsman decked out in period garb. Floor-length gowns and bonnets, cutaway coats and stove-pipe hats – Sherbrooke's a mirror of Victorian life in the good old summertime.

"Everyday life goes on in this actual village," says Family Court Judge Paul Niedermayer, "and down at the courthouse the courtroom is a real one, where actual trials are held regularly."

Judge Niedermayer recalls a day not long ago when Provincial Court

Judge Sandra Oxner, resplendent in judicial robes, sat in that court-room listening to witnesses and lawyers for hours on end. Several RCMP officers were present in court, some as witnesses and others as attendants, and throughout the proceedings droves of tourists drifted in for a look-see.

Midway through a trial, a man decked out in short pants, sneakers, and a multicoloured shirt dropped in to visit. He gazed around the court-room, jaw agape, then stood in the doorway and bellowed: "Hey, Mabel, come on in here – there's a real play goin' on!"

Halifax lawyer Henry J. Dietrich was in that courtroom a few years ago, defending a man charged with indecently assaulting a sixteen-year-old girl. A throng of tourists, armed with cameras, sat in the balcony and followed the trial with great interest. They'd been told not to take pictures, as that was contempt of court.

The complainant testified that the accused drove her to the end of a wharf when the tide was out. She said he parked the car in such a way that if she got out she'd fall twenty feet to the rocks below. Then, she said, he had his way with her.

In the middle of her cross-examination, the girl broke down and admitted that the whole thing was a lie.

"All of a sudden," Dietrich said, "the girl's mother ran up and grabbed her daughter and started whacking her in the head. The judge didn't know what to do. He told the police to get the woman off the girl, and in the meantime the tourists were taking pictures of all of this! Then the judge told the police to leave the woman alone and stop the tourists from taking pictures. What a scene!"

Judge Patrick H. Curran of the Provincial Court of Nova Scotia sends this rough-and-tumble tale:

"When I was in practice, one of my clients was a woman who had a prolonged custody dispute with her estranged husband. She also had a mouth as big as the St. Lawrence River. When we finally got into court she couldn't restrain herself whenever one of her husband's witnesses said anything favourable to his cause. She kept loudly interjecting things like, 'He's lying, Your Honour,' despite His Lordship's (and my) many attempts to keep her quiet.

"When the judge's temper seemed about to break, I turned to her and told her she had better wait outside the courtroom. She accepted my advice, after a fashion.

"As she walked to the courtroom door she had to go past her husband, who had the aisle seat in the rear row. Just as she reached him, she wound up with all her might and kicked him in the stomach. He gasped and turned so white I thought he was going to collapse, but he never said a word about it.

"Apparently I was the only person who saw the encounter. The husband's lawyer, a rather assertive fellow himself, undoubtedly would have made hay out of the incident. However, not a word was said and the wife was eventually granted custody. I think the husband will inherit the earth."

As the saying goes, it takes all kinds to make a world. Judge Norris Weisman, of the Provincial Court (Family Division) in Toronto, glanced down from the bench one day in 1984 and did a double-take. "A father was in court holding a squirmy and squawky infant on his knee," Judge Weisman writes. "To quiet her down, he reached in his mouth, pulled out his upper denture, and gave it to her to use as a pacifier!"

Cornwall, Ontario, lawyer Thomas R. Swabey, who served on the Provincial Court (Criminal Division) in Ottawa before returning to practice, tells of a case tried several years ago by one of his former colleagues on the bench. The accused, a post office employee, was charged with stealing pornographic magazines from the mails.

After a number of mail thefts had gone unsolved, postal authorities and the Ottawa police hatched a plot to nab the culprit. A batch of porno mags were removed from the mail and piled in a special room at the post office. Police sprinkled the entire pile with a chemically treated powder which, when touched, would leave the fingers stained with a purple dye that was almost impossible to wash off. The accused was charged when he was seen walking around with purple hands.

The Crown filed as Exhibit 1 a box of pornographic magazines. At the midmorning recess, the judge instructed the court clerk to bring the box to his office. He hadn't yet heard a word of evidence about the powder that had been used by police.

"The judge thumbed through the magazines while having his coffee," Swabey reports, "only to discover at the end that his hands were covered with indelible purple ink. No matter how hard he tried to wash the tell-tale ink from his hands, he couldn't. He had to return to court with his hands behind his back so no one would realize what had happened during the adjournment."

Sydney, Nova Scotia, lawyer David Muise tells about the time a woman hauled her husband into Family Court for "insulting" her. "In Cape Breton," Muise explains, "an 'insult' is a cross between an insult and an assault." The woman complained that her husband, suspicious that she was two-timing him, took her false teeth and hid them.

Muise, a great storyteller, makes you feel you were there. Here, in one act, is his rendition of the testimony:

JUDGE ROBERT FERGUSON: All right, dear, tell me your story.

WIFE: That husband of mine did the worst Jesus thing that a man could ever do to a woman! I likes to go out to bingo a couple of nights a week and he took me teeth and hid them. I'm goddamn near starvin' to death! All I've had to eat this week is a couple of soft-boiled eggs.

(Husband takes stand.)

JUDGE: You heard what your wife said. Did you do what she said you did?

HUSBAND: Yes, Your Honour, I hid her teeth. I think she's screwin' around on me. She says she's goin' out to bingo but she never brings home any money, so she can't be winning, and the only way I could keep her in the house was to hide her teeth.

JUDGE (to wife): Is that true?

WIFE: That's true, Me Honour, I goes to the bingo, but I'm not screwin' around. Bingo's the only entertainment I get.

JUDGE (to husband): Well, you give her teeth back and she'll promise she won't go out. Now where are her teeth?

HUSBAND: We live just outside town in a cottage that isn't finished yet. I put them up in the rafters.

WIFE: You son of a whore! I tore that place apart for two days and they're right above me Jesus head the whole time!

JUDGE (smiling): Thank you very much. Next case.

"The funniest case I've ever had was in the Small Claims Court," says David Muise. "I call it 'The Case of the One-Eyed Pope.'"

In 1985 a man with a Polish surname died in Sydney, Nova Scotia. His widow thought that, since the Pope was also Polish, it would be fitting to have the Pontiff's face engraved on her husband's tombstone. She went to a monument company, showed a head-on picture of the Pope, said that was what she wanted, and paid in advance for the job.

"When the lady went out to the graveyard to see the tombstone," Muise said, "the Pope had only one eye. There was no way she was going to pay the full price for it. She instructed me to sue the monument company and get some of her money back."

In court, the lady showed the judge the picture she'd left with the man at the monument company. She also showed a drawing the fellow did for her of what the tombstone would look like. In that drawing, the Pope had two eyes. So how come the Pope she was presented with had only one eye?

"My client said she was completely unsatisfied," Muise recalled. "It was an embarrassment. She said she couldn't visit her husband's grave because she'd cry every time she saw the buggered-up job."

Suddenly there was a loud, rumbling sound as two men from the defendant company, pulling on ropes, hauled the tombstone into court on a creaking wooden dolly. As it ground to a stop, so did all talking. Everyone craned to see the tombstone. Sure enough, the Pope had only one eye.

"What's wrong with that?" asked one of the men from the company. "It's a profile, and a nice one, too."

"But I didn't *want* a profile," the plaintiff protested. "I wanted the full face."

"They had a hilarious time trying to mark the tombstone as an exhibit," Muise said, "and the judge allowed my client $150 for the missing eye."

When exhibits are filed at a trial, they have to be retained in the court office for thirty days after the case has been heard. If the losing party appeals the decision, the exhibits are readily available to show the higher court.

"It wasn't long before everyone in Sydney knew about the one-eyed Pope," Muise said, "and for the next month, if you went into the tiny office of the Small Claims Court, you had to step over that tombstone to file papers or do whatever else you were there for."

In 1986 David C. Day, Q.C., of St. John's, Newfoundland, had a case he'll remember for a while. Day acted for a woman who petitioned for a divorce, alleging that her husband had taken another woman to Spain and there committed adultery with her.

The husband popped in and out of the hearing but finally knuckled down to the business of being cross-examined by his wife's lawyer. Let's have a look at the transcript:

Q. Are these allegations which I have just read true?
A. I don't know. What's adultery?

Q. Adultery, Mr. Edwards, simply stated, is sexual intercourse between persons of opposite genders while one or both of them are married. Did you commit adultery?

A. I don't know. What's sexual intercourse?

Q. Sexual intercourse? You don't know . . . you want me to explain to a thirty-eight-year-old man who's been married thirteen years what constitutes intercourse? You want me to? Now, well, then, sexual intercourse is a physical act between a man – you may be an example – and a woman such as your wife, in which the man inserts his protuberance, that is, his penis, into the woman's receptacle – her vagina. Got the picture now, or must I demonstrate and have Her Lady (the trial judge, Madam Justice Mary E. Noonan) take a view?

A. Oh, that's what it is.

Q. Look here, Mr. Edwards. You had three children of your marriage to your wife. How did they come about?

A. I assume I am the father of the three children.

Q. What? You assume? What are you saying? What? Monstrous. This is reprehensible. So we put you down as saying your three children were fathered by another man while you lived with your wife? They are illegitimate children? They're . . . they're products of bastardy?

A. I guess so. I don't know. I imagine so. I suppose so. Yes, I . . . I probably am the father.

Q. Look, Mr. Edwards, very simply this, did you have sexual intercourse with the person named?

A. I can't remember.

Q. After you and your wife separated, did you go to Grand Falls and keep company with the person named?

A. Yes.

Q. Did you sleep with her on any of those occasions?

A. I can't remember if she had a separate room or not.

Q. Did you take your three children on one or two of those visits to see her in Grand Falls?

A. My children never saw us together in bed there.

Q. So you *were* in bed with her, but, of course, you took the sensible precaution of not letting your children see you together there?

A. I can't remember.

Q. What was the nature of your relationship with the person named?

A. I don't . . . it was a friendship. We went out. We were two people who went out.

Q. Did you ever have sex with her when you went out?

A. I don't remember specific occasions. We never discussed it.

Q. When you didn't go out, did you have sex with her in any of the rooms in her place?

A. I have no idea.

Q. Last spring, did you go to Spain?

A. I would suppose.

Q. How did you get there?

A. I flew.

Q. By what airline?

A. I suppose I went in an aircraft.

Q. That's a helpful revelation, Mr. Edwards. Now, did the person named go with you?

A. I don't know. There were a lot of people on the plane.

Q. Who sat in the seat beside you on the way to Spain?

A. Which side?

Q. Either side.

A. Search me.

Q. Mr. Edwards, I'll contact the airline, obtain the manifest, and subpoena all 250 passengers and crew if need be and ask for costs.

A. Well, I know some people on the plane. They looked like Newfoundlanders.

Q. How perceptive. So you went to Spain?

A. Yes, I believe I went yesterday.

Q. And returned on the Concorde, I suppose, to be here today?

A. I have no idea.

Q. And when you reached Spain, did you stay in a hotel?

A. I had to stay somewhere. I just didn't wander around all night.

Q. Speaking of the night, while you were in Spain, where did you sleep?

A. In a bed.

Q. Was there any other human being in the bed with you?

A. There were girls, chamber maids. They came around in the morning.

Q. Did you ever wake up at night and discover, look here, what is this, a woman in bed with me?

A. There may have been someone under the sheets. A hump or something.

Q. We are making progress, Mr. Edwards.

A. I'm leaving now.

Q. Where? For Spain again? By the way, what group did you go to Spain with?

A. I don't know what group I went with.

Q. And you slept in a bed in a hotel?

A. It may have been a motel.

Q. Or motel, and on some nights, something else, another human body, was in the bed with you?

A. Maybe. I don't know. I didn't lie awake in the bed all night.

Q. On how many nights?

A. Three or something.

Q. Which three nights did that happen?

A. I have no idea what three nights.

Q. How long did you stay in Spain?

A. I don't know how long I stayed there when I was there. I don't even know in what year that was.

DAVID DAY: I ask for an adjournment, My Lady, to consider where I go from here. I'll need two weeks.

THE COURT: Very well, the matter is adjourned until . . .

RESPONDENT: Okay. I'll change my mind. I bet you're pleased with yourself, Mr. Day. The answer is yes.

With this concise admission of adultery, Day obtained a decree of divorce for his client. Simple, eh?

2

Let's Hear It for Witnesses

Back in the 1950s and '60s the late Henry Bull, Q.C., was the top prosecutor in Toronto. He was a fierce competitor and a relentless cross-examiner who delighted in skewering a witness, then chewing him up and spitting him out on the courtroom floor. Like so many of his brethren at the bar, Henry also enjoyed a good laugh.

One day, a man charged with indecent assault took the stand in his own defence. When he'd given his testimony-in-chief, he gulped nervously and turned to face the ferocious Henry Bull.

Henry clicked into high gear immediately, seeking to establish that on the night in question the man was the aggressor throughout. The dialogue went as follows:

Q. You met the complainant at the dance?
A. Yes.
Q. Did you ask her to dance?
A. Yes.
Q. So it was *your* idea to dance?
A. Yes.
Q. And you left the dance together?
A. Yes.
Q. Who suggested that?
A. I did.
Q. And you and the complainant went to your place?
A. Yes.
Q. Whose idea was that?
A. Mine.

Henry Bull loved to tell that story, even though he was the butt of it. He knew the importance of taking one's work, but not oneself, seriously. Laughter was important to him, too, because he knew that, without it, a fellow in a stressful occupation such as his could easily slip his trolley.

Let's hear it for witnesses. They're absolutely indispensible to trials (only *people* can tell us what happened), and from time to time they deliver lines that make us giggle, snicker, titter, chortle, chuckle, or guffaw. This momentary mirth is therapeutic, especially when it isn't premeditated. And the witness box is one of the best places to find it.

Witnesses are usually nervous and frightened. Many are scared to death. Unless they've testified before, they're ill at ease, often intimidated by the trappings of the court–the gowned judge peering down from the bench, the court officials, the uniformed policemen, the gowned lawyers asking questions, questions, questions. Folks who are suddenly thrust into this environment sometimes blurt out things they can't believe they've said.

In an indecent exposure case, for example, a woman was asked, "And what did you see when the accused pulled down his pants?"

"It looked like a penis," she said, "only smaller."

A further example: "Have you ever had any other accidents?"

"No, but I had a baby once."

Though most witnesses who say humorous things are accidentally funny, some are deliberately so. Regina lawyer Morris C. Shumiatcher, Q.C., writes, "In a matrimonial case I recently tried, my client, the wife, was being vigorously cross-examined by Tony Merchant, who represented the husband." The following questions and answers appear in the transcript of trial:

Q. When did your father-in-law die?
A. June of 1982.
Q. Are you sure it wasn't July?
A. Well, I hope not, because we had the funeral in June.

In another western case, we have this dandy dialogue:

Q. Are you married?
A. No, I'm divorced.
Q. What did your husband do before you divorced him?
A. A lot of things that I didn't know about.

The pent-up frustrations of long-suffering wives can often be detected in trial transcripts. In a divorce case heard about twenty years ago by Alberta Chief Justice C. C. McLaurin, we get this snippet from the evidence of the plaintiff wife:

Q. What about your husband's looking after the children?
A. Everything would have been all right if he had looked *before* the children.

Here's another woman on the subject of kids:

Q. You say you have had three children. Who was the father of your children?

A. Well, our pastor is the father of the little one.

Q. Who is the father of the others?

A. Our assistant pastor is the father of the next one.

Q. Who is the father of the eldest one?

A. Well, sir, I don't really know. I had that one before I was saved.

Edmonton court reporter Doreen Johnson sends this marital lament:

Q. Would you say that you feel that you made a significant contribution to the marriage by supporting the household while your husband worked in the business?

A. I felt I did, yes. I felt I looked after him. I washed his clothes. He never had to look for a clean shirt. I worked full-time outside the home all the time. I made his breakfast. I washed the dishes. I kept the house tidy. When our house was up on blocks and there was mud everywhere, I went to work every single day, and I brought home water every night and heated it up on the stove for his bath. He got his coffee on time. He'd drink, eat, burp, and go out.

Husbands also know a thing or two about frustration. Just ask a certain Mr. Feigelman:

Before he went on the bench, Mr. Justice Douglas B. MacKinnon of the Supreme Court of British Columbia practised mostly in the field of automobile law. Because he'd never had a divorce case, he boned up on the procedure involved, including a crucial question he had to ask at the opening of the hearing. He jotted down the wording he'd use when asking that question and then went into court for his first look at a divorce case.

The first petitioner to come before him was a stunningly beautiful woman who looked as if she'd been poured into her tight-fitting scarlet dress. She sashayed up to the witness box, then stopped as His Lordship, in a voice dripping with dignity, read from the notes he'd prepared:

"Mrs. Jones, is there a possibility that you and your husband might resolve your matrimonial difficulties and be reconciled?"

The petitioner looked up at the judge and said: "Not a fuckin' chance, Your Honour!"

Hamilton lawyer Patric Mackesy tells of a woman who must have lived next door to the courthouse:

"I was acting for the petitioner in a divorce case based on adultery. The petition had been framed without naming a specific occasion for the adultery. There was to be a short examination for discovery as to the adultery.

"The usual questions were asked, but as an afterthought I asked the lady, 'When was the last time you committed adultery?' She looked at her watch and said, 'Twenty minutes ago.' "

Some witnesses are sticklers for accuracy. Nanaimo, British Columbia, lawyer John D. Hope gives us an example:

Q. Have you lived in Nanaimo all your life?
A. Not yet.

There are, however, witnesses who are not all that fussy about accuracy.

"What's your age?" a woman was asked when being sworn in as a witness.

"Thirty," she replied.

"Thirty?" asked the judge. "You've testified in my court several times in the past few years and each time you've said you're thirty."

"That's true, Your Honour," the woman replied. "I'm not one of those people who say one thing today and another thing tomorrow."

Some witnesses like to keep their age a mystery, as we see in this report from Mr. Justice Anthime Bergeron of the Quebec Superior Court:

"A colourful witness in his late eighties, and looking much younger, was proud of his appearance. After being sworn he was asked his name and address, and then the young female clerk asked him, 'How old are you?'

" 'How old do you think I am, cutie?' he replied."

Cornwall, Ontario, lawyer Thomas R. Swabey, who used to serve on the Provincial Court (Criminal Division) in Ottawa, tells this story:

"Not all profound observations come from those engaged in legislating peace, order, and good government in our country. A few years ago a well-travelled carnival stripper by the name of Chilli Peppers landed in an Ottawa court, following one of her performances at the local fair.

"It would seem that her performance had been as hot as her name implied, and the Ottawa police were not impressed. Miss Peppers therefore found herself wrapped up in the law, if not her clothes. In her own defence, and with a husky voice reminiscent of Mae West, this lady of the world gave the presiding judge something to think about:

"Look here, Judge! You're a cute little rascal! If you and your friends could stop playing cops and robbers all the time you might get some enjoyment out of life!' "

Miss Peppers got some enjoyment out of the verdict – "acquitted."

Vancouver lawyer William M. Carlyle reports that "in the early 1950s I was a junior on a tax case with the late Leon J. Ladner, Q.C. We were involved in an examination for discovery in an income tax case filed in the former Exchequer Court. In accordance with the practice at that time, the discovery was being conducted before the logal registrar of the British Columbia Supreme Court. Our client was fighting a substantial 'net worth' assessment.

"His defence was that his hobby was betting at the local racetrack and that the large increase in his assets could be explained by his track winnings. In the course of his examination he was questioned about his extravagant social life and, in particular, about some of the lavish parties that he was known to host.

"He freely admitted the parties, adding that they were a lot of fun, including, as an example, that 'at one of these parties we had a bathtub full of champagne!' He was immediately asked, in a somewhat sarcastic tone, 'I suppose there was a horse in the bathtub?' My client's immediate response was, 'She was a filly, but she wasn't a horse!' "

Bert Raphael, Q.C., of Toronto recently conducted an examination for discovery of an attractive young woman who'd been injured in a motor vehicle accident.

"Have you told me about all your complaints?" Bert asked as he neared the end of the examination.

"Well, I have pain when I have sex in certain positions."

"What positions?"

"Well . . . uh . . . Never mind, I won't do it that way any more."

W. Wayne Norris, a lawyer in Clearbrook, British Columbia, tells of a mortgage foreclosure action. The woman who was sued was having difficulty giving her address. She took several cracks at it but got no further than saying, "Post office box . . . uh . . ."

"Madam," asked the judge, "are you trying to say that you live in a postal box?"

"No," she replied, "but after this case is over it looks like I might be."

Judge Robert J. McCleave of the Provincial Court of Nova Scotia checks in with this dispatch: "Judge Joe Kennedy of Bridgewater was trying a case of assault in which it was suggested that the plaintiff wife might have replied in kind to the accused husband.

" 'My,' she sighed on the witness stand, 'I'd like to get back to where I was before I was married.'

"Judge Kennedy was sympathetic. 'Just what was that?' he inquired.

" 'I was a widow.' "

Of course, not everyone feels that way about holy wedlock. Vancouver lawyer Frederick L. Ringham sends this tidbit from a recent immigration hearing:

"What is your marital status?"

"Excellent."

Philippe Desjardins of Ottawa recalls a case in which a defence lawyer, who was not the snappiest dresser, asked a Crown witness, "What kind of jacket was the accused wearing at the time of the alleged offence?"

"Something cheap like yours," replied the witness, grinning.

The Silver-Tongued Witness Award goes to the fellow you're about to meet. He testified in a recent trial in London, Ontario, and the court reporter left this record for posterity:

DEFENCE COUNSEL: Your Honour, the defence intends to call evidence. There will be two witnesses – the accused and one other witness who is a long-term employee of the Latin Quarter Restaurant. (Turning to the jury) – Now, ladies and gentlemen, my first witness, a long-term employee of the Latin Quarter, is somewhat slow-witted. You will notice, however, that although he answers somewhat hesitantly, his responses are honest.

CLERK TO WITNESS: Hold the Bible in your right hand and state your name.
        (Witness picks up Bible with his left hand.)

CLERK: Please! Your *right* hand!
        (Witness is sworn.)

DEFENCE COUNSEL: On September 8, 1985, I understand that at 2:30 in the afternoon you were in front of the Latin Quarter Restaurant with another person. Is that right?

WITNESS: Yes.

DEFENCE COUNSEL: What were you doing there?

WITNESS: We were just shooting the shit.

Another London man was charged with assault causing bodily harm. The chief Crown witness, a baker, picked up the accused, who was hitch-hiking near a park at 3:30 A.M. Once inside the car, the accused placed his hand on the driver's thigh. Here's the dialogue between the Crown Attorney and the witness:

Q. What happened after the accused placed his hand on your thigh?

A. I stopped the car and ordered him to get out.

Q. Then what happened?

A. He swore at me as he got out of the car.

Q. And what did you do?

A. I opened the driver's door, got half out of the car and yelled, "You're a fruit! Get lost!"

Q. What happened then?

A. He came around the front of the car. He hit me in the face with his fist. He broke my glasses and chipped my upper plate.

Q. Then what happened?

A. He kicked me in the balls and then ran away.

Q. Now let's review for the jury exactly what happened. You said that the accused punched you in the face with his fist and broke your glasses and your upper plate, then kicked you in the testicles – is that correct?

A. No! No! He kicked me in the *balls*!

In an eastern Canadian city that shall remain nameless, an accused man appeared before a judge who shall also remain nameless. "The fellow went to the detox centre," a nameless lawyer told me, "and when he got out he immediately went to the retox centre – the tavern – where he got loaded. He came back and smashed all the front windows out of the detox centre.

"He was very belligerent in court, and the judge said, 'What have you got to say for yourself, boy?"

"The accused replied, 'Well, Your Honour, like yourself, I'm an alcoholic . . .' "

Gordon J. Kuski, Q.C., of Regina tells of some tough sledding a Saskatchewan lawyer had in a divorce case.

"The lawyer asked his client, the petitioner, if there'd been any collusion or connivance in order to obtain grounds for divorce. The petitioner, the wife, did not understand the question. The lawyer tried to ask the question in several different ways so that his client would understand and be able to answer the question.

"Unfortunately, his efforts got him nowhere and he was met with quizzical looks from the petitioner. The judge finally interjected and asked, 'Have you and your husband done anything to trick the court?' "

The petitioner replied, "Well, we both got lawyers.' "

Victoria lawyer Robert T. C. Johnston relates the problems experienced by a colleague who defended a personal injury claim before a jury.

"The chief complaint was post-traumatic neurosis. A psychiatrist testifying for the plaintiff described the type of personality susceptible to this condition as 'rigid, compulsive, and inflexible.' This fit the description of the plaintiff given by several other witnesses.

"Defence counsel tried to take some of the impact out of this testimony by cross-examining the psychiatrist to show that it was very rare to find these predisposing factors in one individual. The psychiatrist was unmoved and immovable on the point, saying that there were 'whole groups of people who exhibit most or all of these characteristics.'

"In exasperation, and somewhat unwisely, counsel challenged the psychiatrist to 'name one group exhibiting these characteristics.' Smiling at the jury, the psychiatrist said, 'The most obvious example is lawyers.' "

The psychiatrist would, of course, be classed as an "expert witness." A long time ago, an anonymous wag described the expert witness as "some son of a bitch from out of town with a briefcase." This view is shared by many people, judging from the anecdotes one hears in legal circles.

Judge Walder G. W. White of Edmonton tells of an "expert" who sat at the back of a British Columbia courtroom until he was called to testify. When he heard his name sung out he strode quickly to the witness box, briefcase in hand. After he was sworn in, he asked if he could refer to his notes. The judge said that would be in order. The witness opened the briefcase and, looking extremely puzzled, thrashed around among the papers inside it. None of them looked familiar to him. Suddenly, a man at the back of the courtroom stood up and yelled, "Hey, you dolt, you've got my briefcase!"

Crown Counsel Steve Stirling of Port Alberni, British Columbia, is still trying to figure out an answer he got several years ago from an "expert" witness, to wit, a breathalyzer technician. On cross-examination, Steve asked the technician this simple question: "Could condensation in the breathalyzer cylinder cause the piston to stick on the way up?" Here's the fellow's learned reply:

"In theory, if it's hard to come up it would be—I would have to answer yes in that regard, not to beat around the bush, but just to—for example, on a duck, you know—you can take your hand and you can run the feathers down its breast, and it will go real easy one way, see? And then you can take it the other way and run it up the breast and you are going to go against the feathers and you're going to have a harder time.

"You're going to have a greater resistance running your hand up the breast, eh, of the duck, and the only reason I use this description is because I am not sure – I'm not qualified scientifically to know what effect as far as friction or greater resistance – I cannot answer as to this condensation, whether it makes friction equal up or down, or whether it makes it less friction down, or more up. And this is the reason I described the duck."

Professor Robert S. Mackay of the University of Western Ontario fondly recalls the story of a professor from the Massachussetts Institute of Technology who testified in a labour arbitration in Sudbury, Ontario. The MIT man underwhelmed a lot of people.

"What did you think of the expert witness?" someone asked a lawyer who took part in the proceedings.

"The way I see it," the lawyer replied, "there are three things that are vastly overrated – home cookin', home fuckin', and professors from MIT."

Ottawa *Citizen* columnist David Brown remembers a criminal case he covered years ago. "A man in the witness box had a strange speech impediment," Brown says. "He couldn't put a phrase together without using the word 'fuck.'"

The judge tried in vain to get the witness to refrain from using that naughty word. No matter how often the judge denounced its use, the word kept popping out of the man's mouth. Finally, the message sunk in. The witness stopped using the word altogether. But this hampered him greatly in expressing himself, and when he was asked to relate what the accused had told him at a particular time, he choked up and sputtered, "He told me to . . . He said . . ."

"Look," the judge said, "if you're directly quoting someone, that word is *allowed*. But you have to quote him directly. Do you understand?"

"Yes," said the witness. He seemed mighty relieved.

"Now," continued the judge, "what exactly did he say?"

"He said 'fuck off.'"

"All right," said the judge. "Now what did you do?"

"I fucked off."

Many witnesses are much more eloquent than that fellow. Judge Harold Gyles of Winnipeg recalls an impaired-driving case in which the arresting officer said the accused walked "in a somewhat loose-jointed manner."

"What do you mean by that?" the prosecutor asked.

"Well," the officer said, "whenever his feet moved it seemed to come as a complete surprise to the rest of his body."

London, Ontario, court reporter Gail McGilvray transcribed the evidence in a personal-injury case heard in Walkerton in 1985. One of the plaintiff's claims was for loss of revenue from the sale of a book he'd written. Gail figured it must have been a novel because the plaintiff testified, "When I saw the truck in front of me, horror swept my body."

My thanks to another London court reporter, Ellen Vezina, for sending this beautifully crafted reply of a witness in a Manitoba case:

"Where was Tony when Lex came out?"

"Well, after he banged his hands on the truck, okay, he was, you know, sort of, you know – I guess he was just by the trunk there, you know, he hit his hands, you know, on the trunk and then, you know, he's there, you know. You know, what can I say, maybe the rear of the car, you know, the rear corner, you know, of the car, he hit, you know, like, after you hit your hands, you know, on the trunk and then you just sort of – Lex came out and, you know, he moved, he comes too, eh?"

This witness doesn't waste words:

"What do you do for a living?"

"I help my brother."

"What does your brother do?"

"Nothing."

And in a personal-injury case we get this pithy reply:

"How have you been spending your time since this accident?"

"Sitting down."

Maria Kosior sends this report from Edmonton: "A child had been apprehended by the Children's Aid Society and Judge N. G. Hewitt, just before giving his judgment, held up a bottle and told the mother that she was going to have to make a choice between the bottle and her kids. He then asked what it was going to be. She replied, 'I don't drink that brand.' "

Late one morning, Provincial Court Judge Brian C. Stevenson of Calgary sentenced a prostitute: "Fifty dollars or fifteen days in jail. Can you pay that now?"

The woman looked at her watch.

"No," she replied, "but I can by two o'clock."

Mr. Justice Ronald L. Berger of the Court of Queen's Bench of Alberta writes: "Shortly after my appointment to the bench, I presided over a murder trial wherein the Crown relied, in part, upon an alleged jailhouse confession. Defence counsel suggested to the inmate-witness who claimed to have received the confession that his account was pure fabrication. Counsel also intimated that the witness had done this on previous occasions – and always at the last possible moment.

" 'I put it to you,' counsel pressed, 'that you have a history of courtroom deception at the eleventh hour,' to which the witness replied, 'I have *never* been late for court! I'm always there at 10 A.M.' "

You never know what a witness is going to spring on you. William T. Green, Q.C., of Ottawa tells of an impaired-driving case heard back in "the good old days" before breathalyzer tests were mandatory. The cross-examination, by an experienced lawyer, went as follows:

"Constable, there was only a slight wavering over the centre line of the highway, isn't that right?"

"That's correct, sir."

"And when you activated the flasher on the roof of your car, my client stopped immediately?"

"Yes, sir."

"And when he rolled down his window, you detected only a slight smell of alcohol, isn't that correct?"

"Yes, sir."

"And when you asked him to produce his licence he didn't have much difficulty. He was only marginally slow?"

"Yes, sir."

At that point, the lawyer should have shut up and sat down. But he plowed straight ahead.

"Then why did you decide to lay this charge against my client?"

"Because he tried to urinate in my pocket."

In Vancouver a few years ago, a twenty-three-year-old woman was acquitted on a charge of mischief, even though she admitted she'd urinated into a policeman's hat.

"The defence of necessity could be used in this case," Provincial Court Judge Keith Libby said in dismissing the charge.

The woman was being held pending an investigation into the theft of credit cards. Just before she was released without charges, she asked for permission to go to the washroom. She said a police constable told her to shut up.

A constable involved in the investigation had left his service hat in the room where the woman was confined. She said when she was refused permission to go to the washroom, she relieved herself in the policeman's hat.

"Did you try to put the hat back where you'd found it?" the prosecutor asked.

"Yes. After all, I *do* have manners!"

Calgary court reporter Rosemary MacDonald tells of a recent case she was involved in: "An elderly lady was suing an elderly gentleman to get back a deposit of $9,000 she had given him to build a house. Before the plans had been finalized, she backed out of the deal. Before the case got to court, he suffered a stroke and had not fully recovered when it came time to testify. He spoke very slowly and rambled from one topic to the next all morning. Neither counsel nor the court wanted to interrupt him for fear of having him lose his train of thought.

"Finally, with ten minutes to go before the noon break, he summed it all up for us with these words: 'This is all just a bunch of malarky – no, that's a bad word. Bullshit. That's what it is, bullshit!' "

Alan W. Donaldson, a lawyer in Kelowna, British Columbia, reports on a case in which a woman had left her husband and moved in with the owner and operator of a dude ranch. The husband petitioned for divorce and named the man as co-respondent.

At the trial, several witnesses testified that the wife had been prepared to settle all her property claims against her husband for $10,000. The co-respondent had met with the husband to discuss settlement, and now he was being called to the witness box to relate their conversation.

The man was decked out in a red checkered shirt, a string tie, a western belt with a huge buckle, cowboy boots, and blue jeans. He left his ten-gallon hat on a seat in the courtroom when he was called to testify. Let's eavesdrop.

Q. You met with her husband in a restaurant to try to work out the problem?

A. That's right.

Q. And what did you agree upon?

A. Well, I agreed to pay him the $10,000 so he could settle up everything with his wife.

Q. You reached that agreement but you didn't carry it out, did you?

A. No, I didn't.

Q. Why not?

A. Well, you see, I got to thinking that I'd paid more than $10,000 for a good horse . . . and somehow it just didn't seem right after that.

Back in the 1930s and '40s, Henry A. Kurki worked as an interpreter for Finnish lumberjacks testifying in the court of Magistrate E. R. Tucker in the northern Ontario town of Hearst. Tucker "meted out frontier justice in a frontier town," Kurki says.

"A young lady from a farm had accused the hired man of rape," he recalls. "She weighed about 250 pounds. The man was maybe 125 pounds."

At the preliminary hearing, the complainant said that the accused had plied her with candies and chocolates, and she'd yielded her body and had a baby as a result.

Magistrate Tucker didn't believe her and, as the accused didn't have a lawyer, he asked the questions a thorough lawyer would have asked. The magistrate-cum-counsel gave the woman quite a grilling. Eventually she broke down and admitted that *she* had plied the *man* with candies and chocolates.

"Where did this alleged rape take place?" Tucker asked the complainant.

"Oh," she said, "upstairs, downstairs, out in the barn, out in the fields— all over the place."

Mr. Justice William Kelly of the Supreme Court of Nova Scotia tells of a young man in Port Bickerton who was charged with raping one of the local girls. Port Bickerton is a tiny village in Guysborough County, Nova Scotia, where the only employment is in fishing and working in the fish plant. The accused was the son of the manager of the fish plant.

The complainant testified that the accused took her for a ride in his car. "We parked," she said, "and he raped me."

"Are you sure it was a rape?" defence counsel asked her on cross-examination.

"Yes. Definitely."

"Had you ever been out with my client before?"

"Yes, the weekend before."

"Where did you go then?"

"To the same place."

"What happened?"

"He raped me."

"Was that the first time you'd been out with him?"

"No, we were out together the weekend before that."

"What happened then?"

"He raped me."

"What I'd like to know, young lady, is why did you keep going out with this fellow if every time he took you out he raped you?"

"Well, sir, what else is there to do in Port Bickerton?"

Ottawa lawyer E. Peter Newcombe, Q.C., recalls of his first criminal cases, in the early 1950s. His client was charged with receiving stolen goods, to wit, twenty-four head of cattle. In preparing for trial, the young lawyer interviewed the thief at his residence in the local jail.

"Did you at any time indicate to my client that the cattle had been illegally obtained?" he asked.

Mr. Thief considered these words briefly and answered, "No."

Peter was pleased. The Crown would have to prove that at the time he received the animals his client knew, or ought to have known, that they'd been stolen. He'd ask that question again at trial, and, with the answer salted away, he'd be in great shape.

At the trial, Mr. Thief described how he'd stolen the cattle, taken them to the accused's farm, and made arrangements with the accused to rent a pasture for the animals at so much a head.

It was time for Peter to pop the Big Question again. He rose calmly to his feet, like an old pro, and the conversation went like this:

"You at no time indicated to my client that these animals had been obtained by any illegal act?"

"That's right."

"So there'd be no way on God's green earth that this man would know that these animals had been stolen?"

"No . . . except I told him they were hot and he'd better keep them well back from the highway."

48

Mr. Justice Melvin E. Shannon of the Court of Queen's Bench of Alberta tells a touching tale about a divorce case. His colleague, Assistant Chief Justice T. H. Miller, was presiding in Peace River. The courtroom was filled with lawyers, parties to lawsuits, witnesses, and spectators.

After he'd disposed of preliminary matters, His Lordship called the first case on the list of undefended divorce petitions. The lawyer for the petitioner said he was ready to proceed, but when he called on his client to take the witness stand she was nowhere to be seen. No doubt she'd be back, the lawyer said, and the judge put the case at the end of the list.

An hour later, when all the other undefended divorce cases had been disposed of, counsel explained why his client wasn't present. "She's a very shy, nervous person and she panicked," he said. "She couldn't bear to stand up in front of a courtroom full of people and testify about her marital problems."

Miller, a compassionate and considerate judge, was sure the problem could be resolved. He said court was to reconvene at 2:00 P.M. but he'd be pleased to return a half-hour earlier, when few people would be around, and deal with the case in a courtroom free of spectators. Only the petitioner, her lawyer, the court reporter, and judge would be present.

The lawyer thanked His Lordship and returned at 1:30 P.M. with his client in tow. Her name was Mary, and she was frail, trembling, and extremely nervous. The judge invited her into his office and did his best to calm her. Mary finally decided to go ahead with the case. She went back into the courtroom and was sworn in as a witness. The following examination ensued:

LAWYER (in a low, gentle voice): When did you get married to your husband?

MARY (in a low, trembling voice): Two years ago.

LAWYER: What happened after you married your husband?

MARY (always in a low, trembling voice): We got along all right for a couple of months, and then he started to beat me up.

LAWYER: What happened then?

MARY: I left him and went to live with my mother.

LAWYER: What happened next, Mary?

MARY: He came to see me at my mother's house and talked me into living with him again and said he would not beat me up anymore.

LAWYER: What did you do then?

MARY: I went back to live with him.

LAWYER: And how did things go then?

MARY: It went all right for a couple of weeks, and then he started to beat me up again.

LAWYER: What happened then?

MARY: We separated again.

LAWYER: Did he leave you or did you leave him?

MARY: He left me.

LAWYER: How did that happen, Mary?

MARY: I told him to fuck off.

3

"Do You Solemnly Swear...?"

The truth shall make you free.
- JOHN 8:32

O, while you live, tell truth and shame the devil!
—WILLIAM SHAKESPEARE, *King Henry IV*

When you testify in court you have to swear under oath that you'll "tell the truth, the whole truth, and nothing but the truth, so help me God." If you violate this vow you can be sent away for a rather long stretch. Perjury, they call it, and it carries a maximum sentence of fourteen years in the slammer.

With that kind of music to face, you'd think that no witness would ever bend the truth even a teensy-weensy bit. Hah! If you believe that, I've got a domed stadium near Lake Ontario that I'll sell you cheap.

There are many people who have such respect for the truth that they use it only on very special occasions – and court is not one of them. "How can I swear that I'll tell the truth," one witness wondered aloud, "until I hear the questions?" There's a certain logic, and a nice dash of humour, in this observation.

Let's explore this intriguing subject. Let's visit a few courtrooms and see if we can catch anyone in the act. And don't be surprised if you encounter a bit of levity and mirth along the way.

Ottawa lawyer Kenneth C. Binks, Q.C., recalls a criminal case heard in the nation's capital back around 1959. The accused was a man named Roger, who was, as they say, "well known to the court." His reputation for veracity was nearly nil.

The Crown's case was damning and Roger, representing himself, decided to do something about it. He took the stand.

"Do you solemnly swear to tell the truth, the whole truth, and nothing but the truth, so help you God?" the court clerk intoned.

"Oh, yes, I do!" Roger replied, and with that he planted a big, juicy kiss on the Bible he clutched in his right hand.

The Crown Attorney waded into the accused, questioning him closely on his movements at the relevant time, and established in short order that Roger had been at the scene of the crime.

But Roger persisted in denying such a rotten accusation. Every time he answered a question he grabbed the Bible again and bestowed another dramatic kiss upon it. Finally, when the Good Book was so wet it was in peril of sliding out of the witness's hand, Magistrate Joachim Sauvé, a wise and kindly man, leaned forward and said softly:

"Now, Roger, let's have a little less kissing and a lot more truth."

Lisa Keller, a Winnipeg lawyer, appeared recently in an assault case in which she cross-examined the complainant and her girlfriend as to how much drinking they had done on the night of the alleged assault.

"Isn't it true that you consumed so much alcohol that night that you can't actually remember what happened?" Keller asked the friend.

No answer.

"And isn't it true that what *actually* happened was something like this?" Then she put her client's story to the witness.

"The witness listened attentively to *my* sequence of events," Keller reports, "her eyes widening and a smile beginning to grow on her face. When I had finished she stated in a relieved voice, 'Oh, is *that* how it happened? Well, if that's what you say happened, then I guess that's how it happened.'

"The judge, while tiredly rolling his eyes, explained to her that she needn't accept my explanation, that I had merely put a theory before her for cross-examination purposes. The witness then dutifully reconsidered her story and solemnly announced: 'Okay, then I'll go back to my first story.' "

In a similar case, the witness must have thought she was on a quiz show:

"First you said 'no,' now you say 'don't remember.' Now, which one is it?"

"I'm going to take 'don't remember,' because then I can play safe."

Montreal lawyer William Hesler tells of another witness who wanted to "play safe." A long, involved case in the Quebec Superior Court began with a parade of plaintiffs, each one of whom testified after being sworn in by the court clerk. "After a day or two of this," Hesler says, "everyone had pretty well learned the drill, and those who followed were assisting the clerk by pointing out immediately upon entering the witness box whether they preferred to be sworn on the Old or the New Testament.

"Then came the last witness. A man well into his seventies, he entered the box, turned to the clerk, but said nothing."

The following ensued:

CLERK (wearily): Christian or Jewish?
WITNESS: Both.
JUDGE: Both?
WITNESS: Yes, Your Honour. At my age I can't afford to put all my eggs in one basket.

This business of a witness taking a solemn oath goes back to ancient times. Under English common law, which Canada inherited, a witness had to show that he believed in a Supreme Being and had to be sworn according to his custom. It was assumed that a person who believed in God also believed in divine retribution, and presumably would fear that if he lied upon his oath he'd be punished in this world or in the afterlife.

In a famous English case that occurred in 1745, the judge said, "All that is necessary to an oath is an appeal to the Supreme Being, as thinking him the rewarder of truth and avenger of falsehood." Before then, if a witness refused to take the oath or believed that the oath would not affect his conscience, or if he didn't believe in spiritual retribution, he was not allowed to testify.

Today, provincial statutes spell out exactly how a witness may take the oath. The Ontario Evidence Act, for example, says the witness is to swear his oath upon the Old or New Testament by holding a copy of the Book in his hand. (It doesn't say which hand, and it doesn't require any kissing.) If he objects to this way of doing things, or states that that kind of oath wouldn't bind his conscience, he may take an oath "in such manner and form and with such ceremonies as he declares to be binding."

A person who has no traditionally held religious beliefs can, instead of taking an oath, "make an affirmation or declaration that is of the same force as if he had taken the oath in the usual form." Unless these requirements are waived – a rarity – every witness must either be sworn or affirmed to tell the truth before any evidence is taken from him.

In a murder case in British Columbia in 1902, a judge ruled that a non-Christian Chinese man could testify for the Crown if he took the Chinese "chicken oath" instead of the less-solemn "paper oath."

Ah Wooey was on trial for his life. Chong Fon Fi was to testify against him.

The Crown proposed that the witness be sworn through an interpreter in the manner usually adopted in the B.C. courts – by having him write his name on a piece of paper and then burning it, at the same time declaring that he would tell the truth. The consumption of the paper by fire signified the fate of his soul, should he fail to do so.

The defence lawyers said that form of oath wasn't solemn enough, not binding enough on the witness's conscience. They wanted to make it as hard as possible for Chong Fon Fi to fib. They asked that the chicken oath be used, and the judge bought the idea.

The local interpreter, Charlie Loo Fook, and the official interpreter from Victoria, Yip Wing, advised the court that they had discussed matters with Chong Fon Fi and there was no doubt that he feared the chicken oath more than any other. Then the interpreters set up shop. Recalling how things had been done back in Canton, they scribbled the prescribed words on yellow Chinese paper, showed it to the judge and to the witness, and got the show on the road.

The witness signed his name at the top of the document, as required, above a recital of the charge against the accused. Then came the oath itself:

"Being a true witness, I shall enjoy happiness and my sons and grandsons will prosper forever.

"If I falsely accuse Ah Wooey I shall die on the street, heaven will punish me, earth will destroy me, I shall forever suffer adversity, and all my offspring will be exterminated. In burning this oath, I humbly submit myself to the Will of Heaven, which has brilliant eyes to see.

"The twenty-seventh year of the reign of Kwang Su, the sixteenth day, the ninth moon."

Below these words, the witness signed his name again.

Now comes the chicken part, as reported in a law journal of the day:

"The witness having signed his name twice, and a cock having been procured, the court and jury adjourned to a convenient place outside the building where the full ceremony of administering the oath was performed, as follows: A block of wood, punk sticks (not less than three), and a pair of Chinese candles were stuck in the ground and lighted. The oath was then read out loud by the witness, after which he wrapped it in joss-paper as used in religious ceremonies, laid the cock on the block and chopped its head off, and then set fire to the oath from the candles and held it until it was consumed."

Whew! When it comes to oaths, these fellows didn't fool around!

For a while, the judge, lawyers, and interpreters tossed around the idea of having Chong Fon Fi take the "saucer oath." As reported in the law journal, it goes as follows:

"On entering the box the witness immediately kneels down and a China saucer is placed in his hand. He then breaks the saucer by striking it against the railing of the witness box or some other solid substance, whereupon the clerk of the court administers the oath in the following words, which are repeated by the interpreter to the witness in the Chinese language if the witness does not speak English:

" 'You shall tell the truth, and the whole truth; the saucer is cracked, and if you do not tell the truth, your soul will be cracked like the saucer.' "

The judge decided that, nah, that wasn't any stronger than the paper oath and, since the witness had to have the living bejabers scared out of him, he'd better stick with the good old reliable chicken oath.

The Hon. John Arnup, recently retired from the Ontario Court of Appeal, tells a story about an oath involving a plate *and* a chicken:

"Before an important trial at the Old Bailey, it became known that a wealthy Chinese living in London was going to be a witness, and the court officials discussed how he should be sworn. An alleged expert in Chinese law told them that they should have a china plate ready, and a live chicken, explaining that the oath was taken by breaking the plate and wringing the chicken's neck.

"When the trial came on, the registrar explained to the witness that there was available a china plate for him to break, plus a live chicken whose neck he could wring; the registrar said he understood that was how Chinese people took the oath.

"The Chinese man replied: 'Actually, we Oxford men usually affirm.' "

Oh, what a tangled web we weave . . .

Ottawa lawyer Roydon J. Kealey, Q.C., recalls a case in which a bilingual lawyer called a witness who spoke only French. "Dammit," the lawyer said to his assistant, "I forgot to get an interpreter for this man. It's too late now. The judge is waiting for us. We've got to go ahead."

The lawyer asked for a few minutes to speak to the witness. The judge said that would be all right, but he should make it snappy.

"Look," the lawyer told the witness in French, "I'm going to translate for you the questions I'll be asking you in English. I think you'll agree that they're very simple and the answers should all be in the negative."

The lawyer translated the questions and the witness said that, yes, the answers should all be negative.

"Good," said the lawyer. "Now, remember, everything you're asked, you just say 'No.' If you do that, you can't go wrong. Okay, let's get going."

They entered the courtroom and the witness took the stand.

"Do you solemnly swear to tell the truth, the whole truth, and nothing but the truth?" the clerk asked.

"No," said the witness.

The idea of the sanctity of oaths has been under attack for over two thousand years. The great Roman orator and barrister Marcus Tullius Cicero (106 B.C.–43 B.C.) said, "But what is the difference between the perjurer and the liar? He who is accustomed to tell falsehoods has acquired also the habit of foreswearing himself. If there is a man whom I could induce to lie, I could easily persuade him to commit perjury."

S. Tupper Bigelow, Q.C., who was a magistrate and Provincial Court judge in Toronto for nearly thirty-three years, favours abolishing the practice of swearing-in witnesses in court. "No witness except God could tell the truth, the whole truth, and nothing but the truth," Judge Bigelow said a decade ago, "and up to now He has not appeared in my court as a witness."

Though the vast majority of people are probably deterred from lying by the fear of a perjury rap or a dread that the Diety will "nail" them later, there's no doubt that a great many witnesses bend, stretch, and mutilate the truth. There's a whole lot of fibbin' goin' on.

In a case heard in St. John's, Newfoundland, in the 1930s, lawyer Harry A. Winter noted that a certain witness had "handled the truth with penurious frugality." As those who knew him will attest, Harry had a way with words.

So did Mr. Justice James Mitchell (Jimmy) Cairns of the Supreme Court of Alberta. One day in divorce court, in the 1960s, a lawyer said that his client was an atheist and would not take the oath. "Well," said Mr. Justice Cairns, "we'll probably hear the truth for the first time today."

At the opening of the trial of a boundary dispute at L'Orignal, Ontario, a few years ago, Judge Omer Chartrand proclaimed, "I know the plaintiff and I know the defendant and I've read the documents and it's obvious to me that there's going to be a lot of perjury in this case, so I won't swear the witnesses."

If the oath ever is done away with, we'll no doubt be deprived of some humorous moments, for the record shows that witnesses being sworn in sometimes say the darnedest things.

Vancouver lawyer Humphrey E. Waldock sends this example:

Q. What is your name?
A. Omar Demetrovic.
Q. Have you sworn to tell the truth on this examination for discovery?
A. Yes.
Q. What is your nationality?
A. I am a Mohammedan.
Q. Have you just sworn to tell the truth on the Bible?
A. Yes.
Q. Is that okay according to your religion?
A. Sure, I think it is.
Q. Would you prefer to swear the truth on the Koran?
A. No, I swear to tell the truth on the Bible, it is a God book. I swear to tell the truth on anything.
Q. What, even the telephone book?
A. Yes, sure, I swear to tell the truth on anything.

Toronto lawyer Michael Lomer submits this exhibit:

COURT CLERK: Do you swear to tell the truth?
ACCUSED: So help me Jack.
JUDGE: What did he say?
ACCUSED: So help me Jack.
JUDGE: Do you believe in God?
ACCUSED: That's just a name for God – Jack, God, the Creator, the Almighty, the Universe. Do I sound like a crazy man?
JUDGE: Yes.

Gail McGilvray, a court reporter in London, Ontario, sends this snippet:

COURT CLERK: Take the Bible in your right hand . . . No, your *right* hand!
WITNESS: But I'm left-handed!

Cornwall, Ontario, lawyer Thomas R. Swabey, a former Provincial Court judge, chuckles when he recalls the time his court clerk, dazzled by the beauty of a woman entering the witness box, gave these instructions: "Take His Honour in your right hand and listen to the Bible."

Mr. Justice Pierre Michaud of the Quebec Superior Court writes:

"In the district of Joliette, about fifty miles east of Montreal, a dapper and slick Montreal lawyer was pitted against a farmer from the Joliette area. The action pertained to a claim by the farmer against a chemical company that had provided fertilizer.

"When the farmer testified, he was cross-examined by the Montreal lawyer. At every turn he was devastated by the farmer's answers. After a full day of cross-examination, the lawyer looked up at the judge and said:

" 'My Lord, in my twenty-five years of practice, I have never met such an intelligent person as this gentleman.'

" 'Sir,' the farmer replied, 'I would like to say the same thing of you, but, you see, I can't because I'm under oath.' "

Mr. Justice Michaud also tells of a Quebec case in which a horse-racing enthusiast was called as a witness for the plaintiff. The man gave a surprising account of what he'd seen, and the lawyer for the defence began his cross-examination as follows:

"You actually *swear* that that's what you saw? You *swear* this to the court?"

"Yes, sir, I swear," the witness replied. "But I wouldn't bet on it."

When a child of tender years is about to testify, the judge asks questions about right and wrong to satisfy himself that the youngster believes that God punishes those who lie. If the judge isn't convinced the child believes this, the child's evidence can be heard, but not under oath.

Toronto lawyer Garry K. Braund, Q.C., recalls a case in which a little girl was being quizzed about morality by Magistrate "Gus" Thoburn. The dialogue went as follows:

"Do you know what would happen if you told a lie?"

"Mummy says we'd win the case."

4

A Lawyer's Laugh-Along

"In my youth," said his father, "I took to the law
And argued each case with my wife;
And the muscular strength which it gave to my jaw
Has lasted the rest of my life."

–LEWIS CARROLL

Trial lawyers are forever arguing. They're always trying to convince someone – a judge, a jury, a cop, a colleague – that their "pitch" is the only one worth swinging at. Their job is to sway others, to convert them to the view that their cause is right and just and true. They're professional persuaders.

You don't go to a trial lawyer if everything's hunky-dory. You go because you have problems, maybe a mess of problems, and you're hoping like hell that your barrister can blow them away. Your liberty or all your worldly goods might be at stake. Talk about stress!

A trial lawyer's life is crammed with conflict, disputation, and pressure. People who take up this line of work are gluttons for punishment. It's *very* serious business.

Why is it, then, that from time to time one hears of lawyers making jocular remarks in court? How can this happen in the midst of sadness and strain? Are these quipsters heartless swine who revel in the misfortunes of others? Are they completely devoid of sensibilities?

Of course not. Lawyers who dabble in this sort of diversion have learned that the occasional chuckle in the heat of battle helps to preserve their perspective – and their sanity. They know that a dash of humour here and there lightens their load and brightens the road ahead.

Fortunately, the *opportunity* for humour arises fairly frequently in court. Not everyone capitalizes on it, but I'm pleased to report that quite a few do. In this seminar we'll examine the works of a number of Canadian lawyers who – God bless 'em – brought momentary mirth to the proceedings.

Humour can make a sudden appearance even in a murder trial. In St. Catharines, Ontario, an earthquake rudely interrupted the recent trial of Helmuth Buxbaum, the wealthy owner of several nursing homes who was charged with arranging the murder of his wife, Hannah. The ground trembled and chandeliers swayed in the courtroom near the end of the lengthy, sensational trial.

When things calmed down, a woman in the front row of spectators said, perhaps prophetically, "That was the Lord and Hannah giving Buxie and Greenspan a message!"

The occasion wasn't wasted on defence counsel Eddie Greenspan, either. As the quake receded, he turned to the jury and announced: "For my next trick, I will part the waters of Lake Ontario!"

Lawyers learn early that you win some, you lose some. Ottawa lawyer William T. Green, Q.C., remembers the time he walked into court just seconds after a colleague, Dave Casey, had gone down to defeat. Green hadn't heard the verdict and, as Casey was preparing to leave, he asked, "How'd you do, Dave?"

"Not bad," Casey replied. "We came second."

The seats outside a busy Vancouver courtroom were filled with potential witnesses.

"Call Detective Frew," the Crown Attorney barked.

Lawyer (now Mr. Justice) William A. Craig turned to his neighbour at the counsel table and quipped, "Many are called, but Frew is chosen."

Robert V. Blakely, who practises law in Vernon, British Columbia, writes: "When I first moved to Vernon, I was sitting in the barristers' room, where a judge was talking about earlier days in this area when the bar was quite small and very clubby. He said a lawyer came up from the coast for a trial and expressed concern that he wouldn't receive impartial judgment, as the judges and lawyers in this area obviously knew each other intimately and an outsider would have an uphill battle trying to get a fair trial.

"He was assured by the opposing counsel that this was not the case, that the judges and lawyers kept the proper social and professional distance from each other, and that he had nothing to worry about.

"During the trial, the counsel from the coast wanted to describe a particular distance. He said that it was from about where he was standing to a landmark that he could see through the window, but which was outside the judge's range of vision.

"The judge turned to the opposing counsel and asked, 'How far would you say that is?' The prompt reply was: 'It would be about a three-iron for you, Your Honour.' "

The late Joseph Cohen, Q.C., was for many years the dean of the Montreal criminal bar. Mr. Justice Pierre Michaud of the Superior Court of Quebec recalls a time when Cohen represented a politician in a judicial recount of ballots cast in a close electoral contest.

"Mr. Cohen," the judge said, "your client received 124 votes in a polling station that had only one hundred voters. How do you explain this?"

"Overenthusiasm," Joe replied.

Movie mogul Louis B. Mayer, co-founder of the Metro-Goldwyn-Mayer Studio, grew up in Saint John, New Brunswick. Before heading off for Boston, and later Hollywood, he worked with his father, who had a junk business in Saint John. Mr. Justice Rodman E. Logan of the Court of Queen's Bench of New Brunswick tells a story of the elder Mayer that's been told many times but possibly never printed.

Around the turn of the century, Mayer Sr. was sued by a merchant for the sum of twenty dollars. Mayer was represented at trial by J. B. M. Baxter, who went on to become Attorney General of New Brunswick, federal Minister of Customs and Internal Revenue, Premier of New Brunswick, Justice of the Court of King's Bench of New Brunswick, and finally Chief Justice of New Brunswick.

Baxter's opponent was Daniel Mullin, K.C., a colourful, corpulent showman who loved to badger witnesses. Mayer, an Orthodox Jew with a long black beard, had a tendency to talk wildly with his hands when he was excited.

"When you testify," his lawyer advised, "keep your hands behind your back, or keep them in your pockets—anywhere but in front of you. This fellow Mullin is full of tricks and there's no telling what he'll do."

Mayer's hands were anchored in his pockets while Mullin pranced around in front of him, needling him with infuriating questions and enjoying every minute of it.

"Why do you refuse to pay your lawful debts?" Mullin sneered, as he moved his beefy body close to the witness. Mayer's hands popped out of hiding and flailed in all directions as he protested that he didn't owe the money.

Mullin stepped back suddenly and whined, "Oh, Your Honour, Your Honour, protect me from the vicious assaults of me learned friend's client!"

Defence counsel Baxter jumped to his feet and said, "Your Honour, my learned friend need have no fear. It's a cardinal rule of my client's religion that he *must not touch pork!*"

In those days, before movies, radio, and TV, trials were widely attended by the public, and the newspapers gave them extensive coverage. "Baxter Calls Mullin a Pig" was the headline in one of the Saint John papers. And every day, for the next week, Mullin kept dropping in to Baxter's office, with mayhem in mind. But Baxter was never "in."

Few lawyers like sitting around court waiting for their cases to be heard. Judge Patrick H. Curran of Halifax recalls the time Lunenburg lawyer Walton Cook said at the opening of a session of the Supreme Court of Nova Scotia, "Your Lordship, my client has a heart condition and is taking nitroglycerin pills. If his case isn't dealt with right now, I'm afraid he'll either drop dead or blow up."

Calgary lawyer J. Patrick Peacock, Q.C., writes: "Waldo Ranson, a character of rotund proportions and colourful attire, was sitting in a bar in Toronto during Grey Cup week, back in the heyday of the Edmonton Eskimos. A young reporter entered the bar looking for a typical Edmonton fan to interview. After determining that her subject, dressed in green and gold from head to toe, was in fact a practising lawyer from Edmonton, she asked if he specialized in any particular area of law.

"Waldo replied, 'The Law Society frowns on our advising of specialties, but I've always felt the rule was antiquated and I wish to publicly go on record as saying that I do in fact specialize, my specialty being limitations.'

"The reporter inquired what that involved, and Waldo said, 'One thing that all lawyers dread is missing a limitation period, that is, failing to sue before the deadline laid down by law. In Edmonton, if a lawyer is worried about missing a limitation period, he sends his file over to my office – and I miss it *for* him!' "

Back in the 1930s legendary legal wit George T. Walsh of Toronto fought a mortgage action that went on and on and on. It looked as if it would never end.

"How long are you going to pursue this case?" asked an exasperated judge.

"My Lord," George replied, "I'll fight this case to my client's last dollar."

Toronto lawyer Garry K. Braund, Q.C., was on an elevator with Walsh, one day in the 1950s, when a man lit into his wife. "You stupid, no-good rotten bitch!" he snarled. "I hate your guts!"

Braund frowned and shook his head with disapproval. He was about to tell the man a thing or two when Walsh put a friendly hand on his shoulder and said, "Now, now, my young man, never interfere with domestic fights. Over the years I've found that they've always kept shingles on the roof and bread on the table."

Mr. Justice Douglas B. MacKinnon of the Supreme Court of British Columbia relates the following tale:

"Hugh McGivern and Charlie Tysoe are now both dead. McGivern had a warm personality, liked to drink, and was loved by all. He was an extremely talented criminal lawyer. Tysoe was the 'dean' of insurance defence lawyers and my senior partner for many years. He served for some time on our Court of Appeal.

"Hugh was a little out of his specialty. He was representing a seventy-three-year-old man injured in a car accident. Liability was admitted. The only injury of any consequence was not in issue – he was rendered impotent as a result of the collision.

"At examination for discovery, the plaintiff admitted to sexual intercourse once a year. Tysoe offered McGivern five thousand dollars – in the 1950s a substantial amount. McGivern wanted ten thousand.

"The jury trial was very short. At that time in British Columbia, defence opened to the jury. I thought Tysoe was brilliant.

"Then McGivern made the shortest jury address I had heard before, or have heard since:

" 'Ladies and gentlemen, my friend and I are talking about two different matters entirely. He is discussing the loss of sex once a year. I want you to compensate my client for eleven-and-a-half months of blessed anticipation.'

"The jury awarded *twelve thousand* dollars!"

Frank Maczko, Q.C., secretary of the Law Society of British Columbia, sends this spicy story from the 1960s:

"I was acting for a young fellow charged with contributing to juvenile delinquency by having sexual intercourse with a girl under the age of eighteen. He was eighteen, and the girl was his seventeen-year-old girlfriend. They were found at four in the afternoon at Third Beach, in

Stanley Park, stark naked, having sexual intercourse – and other sexual delights – in a car.

"After I'd spoken to sentence and explained the nature of the relationship, Cyril White, the magistrate, asked why they were not in school. I responded that it was Good Friday, and the prosecutor mumbled in a stage whisper, 'I hope they're not Catholic!' "

Ottawa lawyer Kenneth C. Binks, Q.C., recalls a rape case heard in the nation's capital around 1954. Roydon Hughes, Q.C., dean of the local criminal bar, asked the complainant, "Did my client use a French safe?"

Crown Attorney Raoul Mercier leaped to his feet, looked at the jury, and with a pained expression exclaimed: "*We* call them *English* safes!"

Mr. Justice William J. Haddad of the Alberta Court of Appeal writes: "Some years ago, the late Billy Bloor was a member of the Edmonton bar and served his community well as a criminal defence lawyer. His short, thin frame and rumpled and wizened appearance covered a keen and active legal mind. Daily he would be seen scurrying from one courtroom to another, wearing running shoes and carrying his Criminal Code and a small bundle of papers.

"It was the practice in Edmonton in those years for a judge of the District Court, of which I was then a member, to sit in chambers once a month to fix the list for the following month for the hearing of summary conviction appeals. An appeal took the form of a new trial."

On one such occasion, Bloor told Judge Haddad that he represented a certain doctor who was appealing two convictions for impaired driving; if the convictions were not overturned, the accused would have to go to prison.

"I ask that both appeals be heard the same day, as late in the month as possible," Bloor told the judge.

"Select a date, Mr. Bloor, and I'll see if I can accommodate you."

"What about June 30, sir?"

"That's a good date, Mr. Bloor, except that June 30 is a Sunday and a judge won't be available that day."

"That's *great*, sir! We'll need all the help we can get!"

Senator Richard A. Donahoe, Q.C., a former Attorney General of Nova Scotia, recalls a County Court case in Halifax in which a young lawyer, now deceased, was on trial for drunken driving. "He chose to appear in his barrister's gown," Mr. Donahoe reports, "and he sat beside his lawyer, who, of course, was also gowned.

"When the arresting officer was asked to identify the accused, he looked all over the court and then said, 'I don't see him here, Your Honour.' I figured that was the end of the case, when suddenly the accused, not to be ignored, waved at the witness and said 'Oh, yes, I am! I'm right here!' "

Vancouver lawyer Wayne Mackie likes to tell how he became known as "The Terror of the Small Claims Court." Here's his heart-wrenching confession:

"I was acting for the plaintiff in a debt-collection action. I put my client on the stand and got him to give the required evidence to establish his case. I then sat down, pleased with myself, and began to jot down some notes for my masterful summation.

"The judge asked the defendant, who was acting for himself, if he had any cross-examination. He did. While he was droning away at my client and I was scribbling away, hearing nothing, I was jolted out of my concentration by my client saying, 'I object, Your Honour.'

"The judge said, 'You can't object. Your lawyer has to do that.'

"I stood up quickly and said, 'I object, Your Honour.'

"The judge grinned at me and said, 'On what grounds, counsel?'

" 'On the grounds that I . . . didn't hear the question,' I answered weakly and grinned back. The court clerk was convulsed with laughter, and so was everyone else."

Court reporter Maria Mihailovich of Hamilton sends this snippet from a case she reported in the Supreme Court of Ontario:

"What does your husband do, by the way?"

"He's a glue adjuster."

"What does that mean? He's sticky on settlements?"

Provincial Court Judge Hazen Strange of Oromocto, New Brunswick, remembers his first case as a lawyer. It was a speeding case, and there was no defence. Perry Mason himself couldn't have won this one, but that didn't stop the very recent graduate from staying up half the night, trying in vain to find something in the law books that would help his client beat the rap.

The big, burly policeman who'd charged the accused had just finished testifying, and now it was time for Strange to conduct his first cross-examination. He didn't know what to ask. As he walked toward the officer he suddenly remembered that one of his law professors had said that the first question asked on cross-examination should surprise and rattle the witness.

The young barrister looked the copper right in the eye and said, "Isn't it true that you are a homosexual?"

Robert B. McGee, Q.C., of Toronto had a distinguished career as a prosecutor. He joined the Crown Attorney's staff shortly after his call to the bar in 1966 and rose steadily through the ranks until, a decade later, he was Deputy Crown Attorney for Metropolitan Toronto. A few years ago, Bob went into business for himself – as counsel for the defence.

In his years with the Crown, McGee worked with hundreds of policemen in hundreds of cases, from petty theft to murder. Anyone who knows him well knows that, in his books, cops were tops and they could do no wrong.

Sheriff's officer Ed McCarroll delights in relating the story of McGee's first case for the defence.

"Bob worked really hard on that case," Ed says. "He went to the scene of the accident, took all kinds of pictures and measurements, and he had it all figured out that things couldn't have happened the way the Crown said they did."

Around five o'clock on the day of the trial, McGee dropped into a pub where McCarroll and a number of lawyers were waiting to hear Bob's news.

"He came in with his face hanging down," McCarroll recalls. "Someone asked him, 'How did it go, Bob?' and then he cracked us up with just three words – 'The cop lied.' "

Sudbury reporter Paul Derro was covering Provincial Court one morning in 1986 when a fast-thinking lawyer brightened everyone's day.

"A greenhorn lawyer self-consciously took his place amidst other counsel awaiting proceedings," Derro wrote in the Sudbury *Star*. "Called to the bar only weeks earlier, the rookie was sporting – and showing off – a trendy state-of-the-art musical alarm wristwatch received from his parents upon graduation.

"Being a novelty at the time, the watch was inspected by all lawyers present, who passed it around before the newcomer strapped it back onto his wrist.

"The judge entered the courtroom and proceedings were called to order.

"In a split-second of silence, the musical alarm blasted off and electronic beeps of Beethoven filled the crowded courtroom.

"With all eyes upon him, the panicked lawyer fumbled with his watch.

" 'What was that?' the judge boomed.

"Lawyer Mike Hennessy jumped to his feet in defence of his friend: 'The *Moonlight* Sonata, Your Honour.' "

Ronald J. LeBlanc, a lawyer in Moncton, tells of a Crown Prosecutor who sometimes got pretty emotional during a trial. On one occasion, Ron reports, this fellow ripped into an evasive witness with such intensity that he dropped a few swear words into the conversation.

"Watch your language!" the judge thundered. "Remember that you're in court!"

"I'm extremely sorry, Your Honour, believe me," the prosecutor said with great feeling. "It won't happen again."

"Well, it better not," said the judge.

The prosecutor redirected his attention to the witness. He took one look at him, then exclaimed: "Oh, Your Honour, he makes me so goddamn mad!"

Chief Justice Allan McEachern of the Supreme Court of British Columbia relates this story about his colleague, Mr. Justice Wilfrid J. Wallace:

"When he was a young lawyer, Wallace displayed the qualities of quickness and wit that are so necessary for counsel. He was appearing before Judge Swencisky, and near the end of the case the learned judge asked a witness a dangerous question. Wallace, fearful for the answer, jumped to his feet and said: 'If Your Honour is asking that question on behalf of my learned friend, then I wish to object. If Your Honour is asking that question on my behalf, then I wish to withdraw it.' "

Kenneth C. Binks, Q.C., of Ottawa fondly recalls a marathon argument his colleague Lorenzo LaFleur made before the late Mr. Justice Fred Barlow, one of the crankiest judges of all time.

"Lorenzo was a great wit," Binks said, "and he appeared often in the Ottawa courts on behalf of the official guardian. This particular day, thirty years ago, Lorenzo sat patiently as another lawyer made a rather lengthy pitch, asking that the court okay something or other on behalf of a minor.

"When the lawyer was finished his argument, Mr. Justice Barlow looked down at LaFleur and growled: 'What's your position in this matter?'

"LaFleur replied, 'I approve.'

" 'Are you asking for costs?' the judge snapped.

" 'Yes, My Lord, one hundred dollars.'

" 'One hundred dollars! One hundred dollars! You only spoke two words!'

" 'Oh, yes, My Lord,' LaFleur sweetly replied, 'but they were *so* well spoken!' "

Ken Binks also tells of a visit that Ottawa lawyer Marcel Joyal made to the office of a judge of the Supreme Court of Canada in the mid-1950s. Joyal, who is now a member of the Federal Court of Canada, acted for the judge's wife in a separation. He brought the separation agreement to the judge for his scrutiny.

The judge turned immediately to page two of the agreement, the page that said how much he had to cough up for the missus. There it was, in disturbing black and white – a whopping $1,800 a month.

After staring at the figure for some time the judge said, "You know, Mr. Joyal, money isn't everything."

"I agree, My Lord," Joyal replied. "Health is five percent."

You'd be hard-pressed to find a wittier, more eloquent lawyer than James William Maddin, who practised criminal law from 1902 to 1944 in Sydney, Nova Scotia. Maddin defended sixty murder cases, losing only two of them to the hangman.

Sydney lawyer C. M. (Moe) Rosenblum, Q.C., who practised with Maddin for nearly two decades, gives a classic example of his former partner's wit:

"When Maddin was arguing a case before the Appeal Court he was under the influence of liquor, to such an extent that he was swaying back and forth on his feet. One of the lawyers sitting at the counsel table moved Maddin's chair to one side so that he would not be bumping into it. After Maddin had argued to the court that his client, though having a criminal record, was not an habitual criminal, one of the judges on the bench said, 'I know what you mean, Mr. Maddin – one swallow doesn't make a summer.'

"Maddin was about to sit down, but the chair was not behind him and he fell to the floor. He jumped up immediately and replied, 'Exactly, My Lord, but, as you've just seen, too many swallows may precipitate an early fall.' "

Alibi is a Latin word that means "elsewhere." If a person charged with a crime can show that at the time the crime was committed he was somewhere else, especially somewhere fairly far off, he's said to have an alibi and must be acquitted because he couldn't physically have done the dastardly deed. An anonymous wag put it differently: "An alibi is when you prove you wuz at a prayer meeting, where you wasn't, to show that you wasn't in somebody's cash register, where you wuz."

D. Reilly Watson, Q.C., a former judge of the Superior Court of Quebec, recalls a stirring, oddball jury address made twenty years ago by lawyer Harold Maloney of Hull.

The charge was rape and the defence was alibi. The accused contended that he'd had nothing to do with the woman. At the time of the alleged offence, it was claimed, the accused was playing poker with some friends, thirty-four miles away. The poker players trooped into court and so testified.

"Ladies and gentlemen of the jury," Maloney said, "you've heard the evidence. My client was playing poker thirty-four miles away. This means that he *couldn't* have committed the alleged rape . . . And if you don't believe that, there was *consent!*"

The fellow was acquitted.

A few years ago Provincial Court Judge C. Emerson Perkins of Chatham, Ontario, found a man guilty of buggery. Addressing the court on the matter of sentence, defence counsel waxed eloquent. "Your Honour," he said, "society must not turn its back on this young man."

5

The Hall of Shame

Q. And the youngest son, the twenty-year-old, how old is he?
A. He's twenty years old.

There's a place for lawyers who ask questions like this. It's called the Hall of Shame. And a popular spot it is, too, judging from the number of barristers banging on the door for admission.

It's not at all easy to get in. The Hall is the exclusive preserve of superstars – intrepid interrogators who persevered, often for many years, until they finally blurted out a truly memorable Stupid Question.

Even then, they were far from "in." Many a worthy prospect has been denied his just desserts because no one took the trouble to nominate him for the Hall of Shame. Those who make it often owe their good fortune to an alert court reporter who skewered a dandy specimen and sent it to the selection committee with a ringing recommendation. For example, the perpetrator of the Stupid Question recorded above would never have been enshrined in the Hall if it hadn't been for the kind efforts of court reporter Laurie MacKay of Fort Saskatchewan, Alberta. Take a bow, Laurie.

Fortunately for posterity, there's a vast army of viligantes out there – lawyers, judges, court reporters, and others who recognize that it's their solemn duty to pass on the most outstanding Stupid Questions to the proper authorities for due consideration. These are the "scouts," whose tireless search for talent often catapults contenders from minor-league obscurity to big-league stardom, the unsung heroes and heroines who stock the Hall of Shame. Without them, there'd be less laughter in this crazy old world. Let's browse a while among the Hall's exhibits.

Digby R. Kier, a federal prosecutor in Vancouver, nominated this S.Q. and it was duly enrolled:

"Richmond is in an area that receives a good deal of wet rain?"

Ottawa lawyer E. Peter Newcombe, Q.C., tells of an examination for discovery in which he took part. A doctor was asked when he'd first had any contact with a particular child, and he answered that he'd been looking after the child "from birth." Then we're treated to this exchange between another lawyer and the doctor:

Q. From birth?
A. Yes.
Q. How old would the child have been at that time?
A. At birth they are not very old.

Sydney, Nova Scotia, lawyer David Muise sponsored this entry:

Q. When was the building constructed?
A. 1980.
Q. And when did you start storing furniture in the building?
A. 1981.
Q. Did you store any furniture in the building before it was built?

Now you shouldn't conclude from this sort of nonsense that the lawyers who asked these questions are dunderheads of the highest order. All it takes for a questioner to be in big trouble is to let his mind wander for a second or two. In the heat of battle, with many thoughts rattling around in your skull, this can easily happen.

Yes, sir, you have to have your brain in high gear at all times when you're firing off questions. If your concentration is broken, even for a moment, you can end up sounding like an idiot. This is universally true; to show you what I mean, here are some ghastly gaffes from south of the border:

Q. What happened then?
A. He told me, he says, "I have to kill you because you can identify me."
Q. Did he kill you?

Q. I show you Exhibit 3 and ask if you recognize that picture.
A. That's me.
Q. Were you present when that picture was taken?

Here's the twin sister of that question: "Were you present in court this morning when you were sworn in?"

And here's a close relative: "Was that the same nose you broke as a child?"

And another:

Q. Now, Mrs. Smith, do you believe that you are emotionally stable?
A. I used to be.
Q. How many times have you committed suicide?

From a military trial:

Q. What, if anything, unusual occurred that evening?
A. Well, at approximately 17:30 I received a phone call from an unknown person – at the time – claiming that he wanted to commit murder, suicide, and go AWOL.
Q. Was he upset?

This lawyer must have led a sheltered life:

Q. Do you have any children or anything of that kind?

And speaking of children:

Q. Do you know how far pregnant you are right now?
A. I will be three months on November 8th.
Q. Apparently, then, the date of conception was August 8th?
A. Yes.
Q. What were you and your husband doing at that time?

How's this for succinct stupidity?

Q. So you were gone until you returned?

And along the same lines:

Q. You don't know what it was, and you don't know what it looked like, but can you describe it?

The next fellow should take a few days off work:

Q. And what did he do then?
A. He came home, and the next morning he was dead.
Q. So when he woke up next morning he was dead?

This lawyer probably needs a rest, too:

Q. Where was the damage to your car?
A. He crumpled my right front fender.
Q. Which right front fender?

When you ask a Stupid Question, you're spoiling for a snappy comeback. For example:

Q. Could you see him from where you were standing?
A. I could see his head.
Q. And where was his head?
A. Just above his shoulders.

And try this one on for size:

Q. Do you recall approximately the time that you examined the body of Mr. Edgington at the Rose Chapel?
A. It was in the evening. The autopsy started about 8:30 P.M.
Q. And Mr. Edgington was dead at that time, is that correct?
A. No, you dumb asshole. He was sitting there on the table wondering why I was doing an autopsy.

Meanwhile, back home, Grant M. Currie, a lawyer in Saskatoon, recalls a case in which a young defence lawyer was cross-examining a Crown witness. The dialogue, which Grant wisely sent off to the Hall of Shame, reads in part as follows:

Q. So you say that the stairs went down to the basement?
A. Yes.
Q. And these stairs, did they also go up?

Toronto lawyer Alfred M. Kwinter was present in Traffic Court recently when a colleague was representing a motorist charged with making an unsafe lane-change by cutting in front of a streetcar. The lawyer cross-examined the streetcar driver thusly:

Q. Were you in the same lane for a long period of time?
A. All day.

Lawyer W. Wayne Norris of Clearbrook, British Columbia, heard this in the cross-examination of a policeman in an impaired-driving case: "Officer, after my client put the breathalyzer device in his mouth, what did he do?"

Oh, I notice the attendants are getting ready to close the Hall for the day. We'd better be getting along. But first, let's have a look at one of my favourite exhibits. It's this one, right over here . . .

A decade or so ago, police raided an Ottawa apartment and charged a large number of women with performing immoral acts for paying customers. The girls had been highly organized. "They had a Polaroid camera to record whatever exercise a customer might wish to partake in," says Cornwall, Ontario, lawyer Thomas R. Swabey, a former Provincial Court judge who presided at the trial. "Police confiscated a great many photographs depicting the private area of a large number of female persons."

That's *all* these candid shots showed – and in living colour! Every last one of them was mounted on a big display board – "four rows of colour pictures of spread legs," Mr. Swabey notes tersely – and it was the task of a rookie Crown Attorney to introduce this smorgasbord of snapshots into evidence.

The Crown called its first witness, one of the girls who'd been arrested. After fumbling around with several routine questions, the nervous young prosecutor carried the big board over to the witness and asked, "Do you recognize anyone in these photographs?"

"Yes," was the surprise reply.

She pointed to one of the photos. "That's Denise."

"How do you know it's Denise?"

"She's the only redhead."

6

Portrait of a Jester

Wally Myers was a handsome devil. Women wondered why he was selling cars when he could probably be breaking hearts on the silver screen – like Errol Flynn, the fellow he so closely resembled. The girls agreed that Wally was even better-looking than the swashbuckling Mr. Flynn.

But Wally was spoken for. He was smitten with Edith Brown, a tall, curvaceous blonde he called "The Big White Rabbit," and Edith was so hooked on Wally that, one day in the mid-1950s, she invited him to share her apartment in west-end Toronto. Wally said he'd be delighted, and he moved in forthwith.

The flame of love burned brightly for a while, then started to sputter. Sometimes Wally returned at night, but more often he didn't. The couple split up from time to time, but Wally kept drifting back. Understandably, his rabbit began hopping around with other men. One day, five years after they'd first hooked up, Edith booted Wally out and changed the lock on the door.

A few weeks later, Wally decided to drop in on Edith – literally – and in doing so he topped any feat of derring-do that Flynn had ever pulled off in the movies.

Edith's apartment was seven floors up, at the very top of her building, but that didn't deter the intrepid Wally Myers. He went out on the roof of the building, dangled his body over the edge, and dropped onto Edith's balcony. He then entered the apartment, where he suprised the rabbit and a huge fellow attired only in jockey shorts.

Edith informed Wally that her friend was a wrestler who'd asked if he could use the apartment to change into his togs for a match at Maple Leaf Gardens. Wally wisely refrained from mentioning that the Gardens was four miles away and that they had plenty of dressing rooms there.

Edith reported the intrusion to police, and Wally was charged with forcible entry and disturbing the peace. He hired an up-and-coming young lawyer named Garry Braund to represent him in court on the charges.

Though Braund had been only two years at the bar, he'd already made a name for himself around Toronto's criminal courts. A snappy dresser who wore a Homburg to create the illusion of middle age, he'd won a number of big cases and saved three men from the gallows. He had a lightning-fast mind, and people liked him because he was always friendly and cheerful. He took on everything that came his way and, extrovert that he was, loved to put on a show. Especially in the smaller cases, where the stakes weren't high – cases like The Queen versus Wally Myers.

Braund argued that, although Wally had been foolhardy, he hadn't done anything unlawful by entering Edith's apartment the way he did. "After all," he told the magistrate, "my client had been going in and out of that place for years. He considered it his home too."

Then, moving his tongue to the other side of his cheek, Braund discussed the charge of disturbing the peace.

"Your Worship," he said, "my client is guilty of that charge – *if* you spell the word p-i-e-c-e."

The Crown Attorney roared with laughter. His Worship did too. All the steam had gone out of the prosecution, and the charges were dismissed.

Garry Keith Conroy Braund, Q.C., has been stirring up this sort of forensic amusement since he began practising law in 1958. Lawyers call it "laughing the case out of court," and, for sure, it's a dying art. It was much more common thirty or forty years ago than it is in the tense legal world of today. Few lawyers these days have even seen it done, let alone given it a try. It involves making light of the case, with just the right delicate dabs of wit and humour, until the judge or jury starts to think, "What the hell, this isn't so serious," and dishes up a favourable verdict.

Cracking up the court comes naturally to Garry Braund, who simply can't resist some of the juicy opportunities for merriment that arise in the course of a trial. He believes that a lawyer must take his trials seriously, but he fails to see why fun can't make a cameo appearance every now and then. His particular preference is for puns. No, it's more than that. Garry Braund is grossly addicted to puns.

Braund once represented a young woman who pleaded guilty to a prostitution charge. To his surprise, the Crown produced a lengthy record.

When Magistrate "Gus" Thoburn had read it, he said, "Mr. Braund, do you realize that your client has seven convictions for prostitution in Montreal and five convictions for the same thing in Toronto?"

"I was not fully aware of my client's past," Braund replied, "but it occurs to me that her record might have some literary merit."

"Why do you say that?"

"Well, Your Worship, it would make an excellent title for a book – *The Tail of Two Cities.*"

Another lady of the night represented by Braund had been set up by two undercover morality detectives. One officer gave the accused a "marked" twenty-dollar bill, then signalled for his sidekick to enter the premises and make the arrest. The woman dashed to the bathroom and flushed the cash down the toilet.

"What a waste of money," observed Judge M. J. Cloney.

"Yes, Your Honour," Braund replied, "it was a great discourtesy to Her Majesty's face, but at least it was a royal flush."

In another case, Garry Braund appeared on behalf of two brothers named Ball.

"Who do you act for?" the judge asked him.

"The two on the left," Braund replied, pointing to a group of men in the prisoner's dock. "Their name is Ball. There's the left Ball and the right Ball."

Lawyers began to whisper back and forth at the counsel table.

"Who's this fellow here?" the Crown Attorney asked, pointing to a man who sat near the prisoner's dock.

"He's the dick who made the arrests," said Braund.

The lawyers at the counsel table snickered and guffawed.

"They're charged with breaking a safe," the Crown Attorney advised the court. Then, turning to Braund, he asked, "What's going to happen?"

"The Balls are about to be bagged," Braund replied, indicating that guilty pleas were in order.

Gales of laughter rose from the counsel table.

The judge yelled for order, then snapped, "There will be a short recess. Braund, come to my chambers right away! You, too, Mr. Crown Attorney."

The three learned gentlemen had some hearty laughs together and shared a pot of tea before returning to the rigours of the courtroom.

One day, early in his career, a court clerk asked Braund to state his name. On a whim, Garry replied, "S-O-L-E, initial R," and the clerk jotted down this information.

A few minutes later, the clerk called the next case and announced: "Your Honour, Mr. R. Sole appears for the accused."

That became a standard joke in the criminal courts in and around Toronto. To this day, when a judge asks Braund to state his name, chances are that the court clerk will smile and say, 'Oh, I know Mr. R. Sole, Your Honour."

The high-spirited Braund likes to kid the clerks, Crown attorneys, and other court officials, and most of them appear to love it. "We can thank Garry for a good many laughs," says Justice of the Peace Peter Breen, who's known Braund for thirty years. "When he's around things often get uproarious."

Before he was a J.P., Breen had been a court clerk for many years. He remembers a case in which he stood up before a crowded courtroom and read out eighty charges of forgery to the prisoner at the bar. When he'd droned his way through half the charges, Braund scribbled a note and handed it up to him. The clerk snickered when he read its message, and for the rest of his marathon monologue he wondered if it just might be true. The note advised, "Your fly's open."

A short time later, Braund went from bad to verse. Near the end of a drug case in which he won an acquittal for a Mr. Marchisi, he quickly composed a limerick and handed it to the court clerk. The clerk laughed out loud and then Garry motioned for him to pass it up to the judge.

Judge Charles Opper broke up, too, then announced a five-minute recess, adding that he wanted to see the author backstage.

"Damn it, Garry, don't pass those silly notes up to me," His Honour admonished. "But it *is* funny," he added, laughing again. The limerick, which Judge Opper still prizes many years later, reads as follows:

There was a young man named Marchisi,
Whose breath, due to drugs, was quite wheezy.
The judge was impressed
By his lawyer's address,
Now Marchisi can breathe much more easy.

Garry Braund is a court jester, if ever there was one, but that's only one aspect of the fellow. He is, indeed, a man of many parts.

Braund was born into a musical, fun-loving family in Peterborough, Ontario, in 1927. His mother, aunt, and several other relatives taught piano, and his grandparents played piano and violin at country dances. Garry's father had a passion for Dixieland music and jazz and, according to their son, "Mom and Dad were always cracking jokes." Sing-songs around the piano, Irish jigs in the parlour, town dances, country dances, lots of jokes, lots of laughter – that's the salubrious climate Garry Braund grew up in. Small wonder that he's had, in his words, "a lifelong love of all kinds of music."

At his mother's urging, nineteen-year-old Garry started taking piano lessons from the nuns at a Peterborough convent. He flew through the exams set by the Toronto Conservatory of Music, and in the one year of 1946–47 he passed seven grades *and* received credit for a year of theory and a year of the history of music.

Braund's next stop was St. Francis Xavier University, in Antigonish, Nova Scotia, where he received a Bachelor of Arts, with a French major, in 1951. After a stint as a ski instructor in the Laurentians, he entered Dalhousie Law School in Halifax, along with a couple of young men who answered to the names of John Crosbie and Richard Hatfield.

During their three years at law school, Braund and Crosbie were undefeated as a debating team, winning the prestigious R. B. Bennet Trophy and having plenty of fun in the process. Braund says that Crosbie was just as funny back then as he is today. Whenever he thinks of those days at Dal, he recalls a story that he loves to tell and Crosbie loves to hear.

Crosbie had had an operation for hemmorhoids and sat on a rubber ring in class. He'd stand up when the pain became unbearable and sit down when it abated. A classmate, Allan Sullivan, who later was Attorney General of Nova Scotia and then a County Court judge, was giving Crosbie the old needle.

"Crosbie," he said, "you were always a pain in the ass."

Though in agony, Crosbie immediately retorted, "Sullivan, it's bad enough to sit on one without having to look at one."

Braund received a Bachelor of Laws degree from Dalhousie in 1956 and was called to the Nova Scotia bar later that year. The course of his life was altered by the man who took his graduation portrait – none other than the world-famous Yousuf Karsh. Garry's mother knew Karsh's secretary and prevailed upon her to persuade her boss to fit the young man into his star-studded schedule.

Garry had heard that Karsh always ended an assignment by stating what he thought of the person he'd photographed – whether he or she wanted to know or not. A few days earlier, for example, he'd done Greer Garson's portrait and then told her he thought she was vain. Next on the list, after this gig, was Dag Hammarskjöld, Secretary General of the United Nations. "Mr. Karsh sure keeps classy company," Garry muttered to himself, marvelling that he'd even been allowed on the premises. He started to fret about what Karsh might say about *him*.

"Now I must tell you what I think of you," Karsh said when his work was done. Braund gulped hard.

"How many people are there in Peterborough?" Karsh asked.

"About thirty thousand, sir."

"And Halifax, where you said you might practice?"

"About ninety thousand."

"You are a very pleasant and likeable young man. You belong in a very big city, where you can meet *thousands* of people."

In 1958 Braund was called to the Ontario bar. He immediately opened a law office in downtown Toronto – near the courts, of course.

Gary likes to reminisce about his early days in practice, "when there were so many more characters at the bar than there are today." They were free-wheeling times, and the likes of Tommy Horkins, Freddie Malone, and Manny Frankel could be counted on to say anything that popped into their heads, no matter how irrelevant or outrageous.

"Manny Frankel and I once defended a couple of fellows in a jury case," Braund recalls. "Manny had had thousands of cases, but I don't think he'd ever been in front of a jury before. Shortly after he started his address to the jury, Manny ran out of things to say. He turned around, looked at me, and said: 'Ladies and gentlemen of the jury, I submit that my client is innocent. If he was guilty, he would've got a much higher-priced lawyer than me. He would've got Mr. Braund here.' "

Braund once asked Frankel, "Manny, have you ever had a murder case?" Frankel replied, "Christ, I've murdered every case I've ever had!"

Moving from one-liners to high drama, Braund recalls a case in which he acted for a former Hungarian freedom fighter who'd pleaded guilty to possessing an offensive weapon. The man was terrified of going to jail.

"Twenty-five dollars or ten days in jail," said the magistrate, who was known for never allowing an accused time to pay a fine.

"My client is out of work right now, Your Worship," said Braund. "Could he have a bit of time to raise the money?"

"No time to pay! Next case!"

"What happens now?" asked the client.

"I'm afraid you'll have to go to jail," Braund replied.

As the man passed the counsel table, he fainted dead away. As he was falling. Braund grabbed his client's glasses off his head, so they wouldn't be broken, and with a flourish asked the court, "In view of the sudden change of circumstances, *now* can he have time to pay?"

"Thirty days to pay," His Worship conceded.

One fine October day Garry Braund was sitting in court, waiting for his case to be called, when he heard Crown Attorney Jim Crossland bawling the living hell out of a man in the prisoner's dock. The man had just been arrested for failing to show up to answer a criminal charge on a previous occasion.

"Where have you been?" Crossland barked.

"I had to go home," the accused replied.

"Where's home?"

"Newfoundland."

"When did you go home?"

"March 3rd."

"Why did you go home?"

"For my father's funeral."

"But that was seven months ago!"

Braund couldn't contain himself. "Jimmy," he said in a loud stage whisper, "it was a long procession!"

And it was a long time before the laughter died down in court.

Garry Braund didn't get along too well with Henry Bull, Q.C., Toronto's top prosecutor in the 1950s and '60s. It might have been because Braund usually topped him in repartee.

To bug Bull, Garry walked into court one day lugging a large medical book under his arm.

"I see Braund has brought a big book with him," Henry said to Magistrate "Gus" Thoborn. "It's probably *Braund on Bluff.*"

"No," Braund replied, "it's *Bull on Shit.*"

"Now, now, now," His Worship said after he'd had a good laugh, "this is no place to talk that way."

Braund has never confined himself to criminal law, although that's the field that has yielded his biggest crop of laughs. He once brought a motion in the Supreme Court of Ontario, asking that a certain divorce case that had languished for a long time be put back on the trial list.

"What's the problem with this case of Smoke versus Smoke?" asked Mr. Justice Dalton Wells.

"I ask that it be restored to the list, My Lord," Braund replied. "I'd like it rekindled."

The judge laughed and said, "What happened to this marriage?"

"Well, My Lord," said Braund, "it was a bad match."

His Lordship called a recess and asked that Braund see him in his chambers. "Please don't make me laugh like that," he chuckled backstage. "You know I've got high blood pressure."

There's method in this man's madness; Braund believes strongly that laughter truly is the best medicine. "It's a form of medical insurance," he says seriously. "You don't get ulcers if you have a good laugh every now and then. I couldn't *buy* an ulcer."

He's always optimistic, always seeing the bright side of things. He puts it rather well: "If I'm in a tough situation, in life or in court, I say to myself, 'I'm going to get out of this.' Some people say I've always whistled past the graveyard. At least I whistle, and sing a merry tune. I'll cry for no man, including myself. You've got to be able to laugh at yourself. If you don't, life can be awfully rough."

The way Garry Braund sees it, humour provides more than a good laugh. It's also a useful courtroom tool. "If it's not overdone," says the fellow who often overdoes it, "humour can establish a good rapport with the judge. In a courtroom, the only place you don't need 'pull' is where you see a door marked 'push.' You need every break that you can get in there, and humour *is* a break. It gives you an edge over someone who doesn't have the gift. Humour breaks the ice, relieves the tension – the way music does."

Though he's busy in many areas of law, Braund's first love is the courtroom. "What I like the most about court," he says, "is that in a trial you have live drama. If there's a tear it's a real tear, and if there's a laugh it's a real laugh. The humour is just as pure and beautiful as the sadness that exists as a balance."

These are the words of a man who's known far and wide as a jester. With Braund, horsing around is clearly only a part-time job.

Long ago, Garry declared war on pornography – what he calls "smut for profit." He says he's noticed over the years that "a lot of serious crimes are committed by men who are avid readers of hard-core pornography."

In the early 1970s Braund helped organize a Canadian chapter of a U.S. organization called "Citizens for Decent Literature," and he served as its national chairman. He's worked tirelessly in the cause, speaking to service clubs, appearing on panels, and giving interviews to the media. He's saddened that the movement has lost ground in recent years to "the billion-dollar business that dumps manure on our kids." Braund says most adults can't be favourably influenced, "but children under fifteen can be. We've got to protect them by passing better laws – and enforcing them."

Right up there with laughter, the piano is one of Garry's best antidotes to the pressures of life and the law. He often combines these therapies by pounding out robust music-hall numbers and singing their outrageous lyrics at the top of his clear tenor voice. He and his wife, Betty, spend much of their spare time around the piano. Sing-songs spring up at the drop of a note, and Garry and Betty are as much at home with Chopin as they are with the old standards, pop music, ragtime, and jazz. Garry has a big following at a west-end Toronto restaurant, where he appears most Thursday nights, playing and singing practically every kind of music known to man. He's also gung-ho about skiing and sailing.

Braund believes – correction, he *knows* – that fun can be found almost anywhere. Even at work. Some days, *especially* at work. In addition to firing off puns in all directions, this irrepressible fellow gets a charge out of dreaming up preposterous "defences" and trying them out on startled prosecutors. A couple of examples will suffice.

A few years ago a pair of Toronto detectives spent many hours spying through a small vent, looking for evidence of homosexual activity in an adjoining subway-station men's room. Finally, their efforts were rewarded. In came two men, one of them quite drunk. The other man opened the drunk's fly, pulled out his penis and . . . the police ran next door and made the arrests.

Garry Braund was retained to represent the owner of the penis. Another lawyer, inexperienced in the ways of criminal law, was hired to protect as best he could the reputation of the second man, who – saints preserve us! – was an ordained minister. Lawyer number two was happy to let Braund run the show. And what a show it was!

"What's the defence?" asked Braund's helper.

"Good Samaritan."

"What? I've never heard of that defence. Are you sure . . .?"

"Look," said Braund, "my client was so drunk he couldn't get his penis out of his pants. Your client was drunk, too, but not as drunk as mine. He had to help my client get his penis out of his pants. Don't you see? He came to his rescue. He was a Good Samaritan."

"Oh, yeah. It *might* work."

"Trust me."

A few minutes before the start of the trial, Garry Braund was loosening up the enemy.

"Is there any fingerprint evidence?" he asked Detective Donny Pogue.

"Yeah – on the fellow's pecker."

"My, my, that would be impeccable evidence," observed Crown Attorney Lloyd Graburn, Q.C.

"Only circumcisional," Braund noted.

Everyone – except the accused – hooted with laughter. The court clerk, tears streaming from his eyes, said that if the miscreants were fined they should have to pay an extra twenty-five dollars "for amusement tax."

Oyez! Oyez! Judge William F. Rogers strode onto the dais, and the trial got under way.

Detective Pogue took the stand and described what he'd seen through the vent.

"I saw this man, in a slumped position, standing at the urinal," Pogue began. "I saw the other man come up and look at the front of the man's trousers and unzip his fly and remove his penis, and then the man relieved himself."

Then the minister testified. He said he could see that the other man was going to urinate in his pants and he decided to help him, so he pulled down the man's zipper, removed his penis, allowed him to urinate, and then put the penis back where it was supposed to be and pulled the zipper up.

Lloyd Graburn asked Detective Pogue to return to the stand. "Have you any comment on what this accused has said?" Graburn said.

"Yes," said the witness, "he did pull the zipper down and he did pull the penis out, and from –"

"Yes?"

"From my vantage point, I saw him pull it thirty-seven times."

"Son of a gun!" Braund recalled later. "The defence of Good Samaritan had gone up in smoke!"

In another case, Garry Braund represented a couple of strippers who'd performed certain services at an all-night stag. The evidence against the accused was given by a police officer who'd watched the girls through a second-floor window. He was hanging upside-down at the time, his legs clutched firmly by two colleagues on the roof of the building.

"As I recall the evidence," Braund said, "a gentleman was lying on his back on the stage. One lady had sunk herself onto his instrument and the other lady was sitting on his head. This is what the officer had seen – upside-down, of course."

Braund dropped in to see the Crown Attorney, John Applegath, a few minutes before the trial was scheduled to start. It was time to jolly-up John.

"You're pleading guilty, I suppose," Applegath said.

"Not on your life!" Braund declared.

"Why do you say that?"

"There's a defence, John."

"*What* defence?"

"Squatter's rights!"

7

Judicial Jollies

Now you might find this hard to believe, but judges are human – just like you and me.

Oh, I know, they usually look so stern and severe, peering down from that lofty bench. But I bet you'd be a bit sombre, too, if you had to listen to all that serious stuff and dispense justice all the livelong day.

"Judgin' ain't easy," a wise man once observed.

That's true. Ask any judge. There's a lot of pressure on you. Someone's liberty or life's savings may be on the line. Everyone's counting on you to come up with "the right decision." The damn trouble is that there's always two different versions of what "the right decision" should be. No matter which one you select, someone's going to think you're a cold, heartless nincompoop who should be drummed out of the judgin' business, forthwith. What a weird way to make a living, eh?

And then there's the boredom. Yes, boredom. If you think that what witnesses and lawyers say is always interesting, you'd better swear off TV and the movies. Most trials don't zip along. They inch along on leaden feet. Why, the judge often has to battle to keep from going bye-byes. What's he or she to do, scream? No, but a giggle or a guffaw would sure work wonders.

Mercifully, laughter sometimes plays a sudden visit to the courtroom, and the tension disappears for a while. A lawyer might make a quip that tickles a few funnybones. A witness might say something that strikes everyone but him as hilarious. Even the judge might crack off a humorous comment or two. It's a lot easier for *him* to make with the mirth; after all, he's running the show.

When it comes to generating a laugh, judges don't have to take a back seat to anyone. Let's look in on some Canadian judges and see how they get their judicial jollies. Please be sure to chortle in all the right places. This is *their* chapter, and I wouldn't want anyone to be held in contempt of court.

Provincial Court Judge Patrick H. Curran of Halifax sends this report: "The first witness in a case being heard by Judge Joe Kennedy (of

Bridgewater, Nova Scotia) was Staff Sergeant White, a firearms expert with the RCMP crime lab. The staff sergeant hadn't had time to get all his files in order before he was called to testify, so he continued to do so when he first got on the witness stand.

"The prosecutor said, 'Officer, would you please give your full name and address.'

"Staff Sergeant White, engrossed in his files, said nothing. The prosecutor tried again: 'Please tell us your name and address.' Still no response.

"Becoming a little agitated, the prosecutor said, 'Give us your name and address.' When there was still no reply, Judge Kennedy interjected, 'Now, just take it easy, Staff Sergeant White. Don't worry, the questions will start to get easier as we go along.' "

District Court Judge Ray Stortini of Sault Ste. Marie, Ontario, chuckles whenever he recalls a case he fought in his early years as a lawyer. It was heard by Judge Harry J. Reynolds, Judge Stortini's predecessor on the bench. Perhaps Judge Reynolds should have been tried himself – for practising philosophy without a licence.

"When I first started practising law," His Honour writes, "I, like many others, really got caught up in my client's cases. One of my clients had taken up with a woman and eventually moved into her apartment. While there he rebuilt her kitchen cupboards, bought new drapes, etc. Then she threw him out. I filed a mechanic's lien on his behalf and we went to court, at which time Judge Reynolds found that it was all a gift and we lost the case.

"Later that day I attended on Judge Reynolds for an *ex parte* order in an unrelated matter, and he remarked that I didn't appear to be too pleased with his judgment that morning.

" 'Your Honour,' I said, 'that poor fellow paid out all that money for those things that she kept.'

"The judge put a kindly hand on my shoulder and in a fatherly manner said, 'Ray, that's the screwing he gets for the screwing he got!' "

Ottawa lawyer James B. Chadwick, Q.C., who's done a lot of referral work for Newfoundland lawyers, tells about a charge of bestiality that was brought against a man in a Newfoundland outport. The man, it was alleged, had been entirely too amorous with his horse.

Court recessed at lunchtime and the sheriff said to the judge, "Should we take the prisoner across the street to the restaurant?"

"No," the judge replied, "go and get him a sandwich. And while you're at it, get him a bale of hay for his girlfriend."

The late Mr. Justice D. C. Disbery of the Saskatchewan Court of Queen's Bench had a wonderful sense of humour. William M. Elliot, Q.C., of Regina recalls a case tried by Mr. Justice Disbery. It had to do with one of the driest subjects a judge could hear – the priorities between a chattel mortgagee and a bank that had received an assignment of chattels as security for a debt.

In his judgment His Lordship noted that some of the chattels, to wit, 401 pigs, had been seized by a bailiff at the post office in Laventure, Saskatchewan.

"Unfortunately," he wrote, "the evidence does not disclose whether the pigs were merely waiting for the mail or demonstrating against the postal authorities."

Judge Walder G. White of Edmonton has a batch of stories about the late Mr. Justice Harold Riley of the Alberta Court of Queen's Bench. "On one occasion," he recalls, "a court orderly came to Harold Riley in a tizzy. He was upset because Riley's big dog, Rousseau, had peed on the courtroom wall in the Court of Appeal.

"Riley just dismissed the matter with a wave of his hand and said, 'It's okay, I've been wanting to do that for years.' "

Sydney, Nova Scotia, lawyer David Muise heard this dandy dialogue in the Provincial Court in his home town:

JUDGE R. J. MACDONALD: I'm sentencing you to fourteen days in jail.
ACCUSED: No problem, Your Honour. I can do that standing on me head!
JUDGE MACDONALD: And I'm adding another fourteen days to get the blood back down to your feet.

On another occasion, Muise, just out of law school, made a memorable appearance before the crusty Judge MacDonald. "I had been up half the night preparing for trial," he recalls. "I'd read all the case law on the subject and I made a very lengthy argument. It went on and on, and while I was arguing, Judge MacDonald was doodling and looking out the window at the ducks in the park.

"I stopped in the middle of my brilliant argument and said, 'Your Honour, are you following me?'

" 'Oh, yes, my boy,' he said, 'I'm following you. But if I could find my way back alone I'd leave you right here!' "

Another Sydney lawyer, C. M. (Moe) Rosenblum, Q.C., loves to tell about an attempted murder case that he and Dave Muise defended a few years ago. Moe, who's been practising since 1927, tends to his clients' affairs for eight months of the year and spends his winters relaxing in Florida.

At the end of the trial the judge, who was known for procrastinating, said to counsel, "Well, gentlemen, we've had four days of testimony and heard from thirty-seven witnesses. It's going to take me some time to review all the evidence and come to a decision. I'm going to consider this matter for a month and I'll render my decision then."

Rosenblum was having none of this. He rose quickly to his feet and said, "As Your Honour knows, it's almost Christmas and I go to Florida for the winter."

"All right," said the judge. "Guilty!"

Mr. Justice Anthime Bergeron of the Superior Court of Quebec relates some recent dialogue between his colleague, Mr. Justice Pierre Michaud, and a man who'd been brought into court on a matrimonial matter.

"Are you represented by a lawyer?" Mr. Justice Michaud inquired.

"Jesus Christ is my lawyer," the man replied.

"You certainly have a good one," His Lordship observed, "but don't you think you should have a member of the *local* bar?"

Rene Monty, a retired Quebec lawyer now living in Florida, recalls a case in which a woman witness, "easily past fifty," was asked by the court clerk to state her name, address, and age. She obliged on the first two matters but balked at revealing her age.

"What's *your* guess?" she said to the judge.

The judge smiled courteously and told the clerk, "Put down thirty-nine."

Sine die is a Latin expression that crops up frequently in the courts. It means, literally, "without date." When a case is adjourned *sine die*, it's postponed indefinitely. Chief Justice Allan McEachern of the Trial Division of the Supreme Court of British Columbia has a story about that expression:

"Mr. Justice Albert Mackoff has one of the quickest wits on the bench or at the bar. A young lawyer once applied in chambers before Mr. Justice Mackoff for leave to issue a subpoena on a non-citizen who resided out of the province. Mr. Justice Mackoff doubted that the court had this jurisdiction, a question that never crossed the fertile mind of this young counsel. The lawyer pressed for an order, but Mr. Justice Mackoff continued to doubt the jurisdiction.

"Finally, the young man asked if his application could be adjourned so that he could get further authorities.

" 'To what date?' inquired the judge.

" 'Oh, *sine die*,' said the lawyer, to which Mr. Justice Mackoff replied, 'Don't you think *sine die* is a trifle too soon?' "

Corpus delicti is another Latin term that's tossed around a lot. It does not mean a corpse, as many people believe, but "the body of a crime," a substantial fact that proves that a crime has been committed.

Bob Prince, a lawyer in Yarmouth, Nova Scotia, recently heard two men plead guilty to a charge of theft of a pig. After hearing the facts, the judge asked what had become of the pig. "We ate it," one of the men replied.

The judge smiled, then said to the prosecutor, "It's fortunate for you that the accused entered guilty pleas. Otherwise, the Crown would have had no *porcus delicti*."

Senator Richard Donahoe, who practised law for many years in Halifax and is a former Attorney General of Nova Scotia, recalls a humorous conversation he once had with a friend. "He told me that the night before, a lady's name came into the conversation and everyone present was asked if they could recall her maiden name," the senator writes. "No one could, but then my friend said, 'I remember now. She was a Pye, and a nice piece, too.' "

Some time later, Donahoe appeared before Judge R. H. Murray of Halifax. He was seeking an adoption order for a client named Pye. "I told my story about Miss Pye who was a nice piece and, as quick as a flash, Judge Murray said, 'You don't suppose she was a tart, do you?"

Durham, Ontario, lawyer Peter Fallis tells of a case in which District Court Judge Donald Thompson of Owen Sound had to wrestle with the wording of a contract, specifically paragraph 2, subclause (b) thereof. One lawyer argued that that provision of the agreement applied, so his client should win the case. The other lawyer said it didn't apply and *his* man should be the winner.

"Gentlemen," Judge Thompson declared, "this is a clear case of 2(b) or not 2(b)."

John G. (Jake) Dunlap, Q.C., of Ottawa recalls a divorce case heard in the early 1960s by the ever-witty Mr. Justice George T. Walsh of the Supreme Court of Ontario. The plaintiff's lawyer had taken up a great deal of the court's time but hadn't come close to proving adultery.

"Do you have any evidence of adultery?" Mr. Justice Walsh inquired hopefully.

"Oh, yes, My Lord," the lawyer replied, "*Oceans* of it."

His Lordship leaned forward and said gently, "Then give me a trickle of it, will you?"

At about the same time, in a divorce case in Alberta, the defendant admitted that he'd committed adultery three times in one day. It is reliably reported that the trial judge, Mr. Justice James (Jimmy) Cairns, removed his spectacles and muttered, "Magnificent!"

Mr. Justice Melvin E. Shannon of the Court of Queen's Bench of Alberta has preserved this pearl for posterity:

"A very earnest, serious counsel appeared before the late Justice Jimmy Cairns. He was there to assess damages in a personal injury case. After the evidence had been heard, the earnest counsel for the plaintiff presented his argument to Justice Cairns and, as is customary, said everything he could to persuade the judge that a substantial award was appropriate. At one point he proclaimed, 'I am sure that your Lordship does not know how serious it is to have an atrophied muscle.'

"Mr. Justice Cairns replied, 'I do not know how serious it is, but I do know how embarassing it is.' "

Federal prosecutor Brian Purdy, Q.C., of Vancouver has a great story about the late Mr. Justice Allen Cullen of Alberta "back in the days when he was a District Court judge." Here it is, in Brian's own colourful words:

"I met Judge Cullen on the street outside the Land Titles Office, and we fell into a discussion of a robbery trial I had completed before him a few days earlier. While we were talking, a flight of pigeons took off from the Land Titles Office and soared over our heads.

"The pigeon squadron came in from behind me. One of them released a precision shot that passed over my head without touching me but adorned Judge Cullen from the top of his hat, which he was fortunately wearing, down the front of his topcoat. Because Judge Cullen was talking at that moment he did not notice what had happened, but he soon gathered that something was afoot by the horrified expression on my face. I was, after all, a very junior lawyer talking to a judge who had just been dumped on from above.

"I was frantically groping for an appropriate comment when Judge Cullen demonstrated the difference between junior lawyers and judges, and showed why he was so warmly regarded by the Alberta bar as a wit and raconteur. He looked down, saw the unfortunate evidence, then looked to the heavens and said, 'For some people they sing.' "

In a Nova Scotia case a few years back, a man accused of break, enter, and theft took the witness box. He was no stranger to the court. After stating his name and address, he was asked his occupation.

"Crook!" snapped the judge, before the man could move his lips.

When a judge renders a decision, "reasons for judgment" are usually stated in detail. Some judgments run to dozens of pages. A decade ago three judges of the British Columbia Court of Appeal heard argument in a case, and one of the judges, Mr. Justice Hugh Alan Maclean, indicated that the appeal would have to be dismissed.

Chief Justice Allan McEachern of the Trial Division of the Supreme Court of British Columbia describes what followed: "Disappointed but courageous counsel inquired if reasons for judgment could be given. 'Very well,' said Mr. Justice Maclean, and he called for the court reporter. When all was ready, His Lordship delivered a most penetrating and closely reasoned judgment: 'This appeal is dismissed because it *should* be dismissed. The court will now adjourn.' "

Toronto lawyer Russell Otter, Q.C., tells of a time he appeared before Provincial Court Judge Robert Dnieper, affectionately known as "The Sniper." Otter was representing a woman charged with a driving offence.

"Your Honour, my name is Otter and I rep . . ." Russ began.

"Just a minute!" snapped the judge. "Is the investigating officer here?"

"I don't see him, Your Honour," a policeman answered.

"Go look in the hall," the judge ordered.

The policeman went out and looked. A minute later, he returned. "He's not there."

"Stand up, Mrs. Smith," Judge Dnieper directed. Nervously, the accused rose to her feet.

"The officer's not here, so there's no evidence against you. I'm dismissing the charge. You can go now."

"Oh, thank you, Your Honour."

"You're welcome."

Then, turning to Otter, the judge said, "Masterful performance, counsel."

"Thank you, Your Honour."

"You're welcome."

Lawyer and client started to leave.

"By the way, Mrs. Smith . . ."

"Yes, Your Honour?"

"I hope your lawyer charges by the word."

On another occasion Judge Dnieper convicted a young man who'd damaged some property. His girlfriend had jilted him, so he got drunk and went on a bit of a rampage. The judge felt sorry for the fellow, who was still pining for his girl, and he gave him this fatherly advice: "Son, women are like a Queen Street streetcar. There'll be another one along in a few minutes."

Toronto lawyer David P. Cole writes, "Judge Robert Dnieper has legendary wit. I once represented a young man before His Honour in Bail Court. After losing the bail hearing, the accused took umbrage and threw a book at me. After the accused was removed from the court, I picked up the book. The following dialogue ensued between Judge Dnieper and me:

"Counsel, what's that?'

" 'It's the New Testament. Being Jewish, I have no use for it. Would Your Honour like it?'

" 'No, Counsel, I am already fully familiar with the contents.'

" 'What should I do with it?'

" 'Counsel, I suggest you read it as carefully as you would the amendments to the Criminal Code.' "

Former Ontario Chief Justice G. A. Gale recalls a civil case he once tried, Jones versus The Sisters of St. Theresa. At the opening of the trial, noted Toronto counsel Isador Levinter, Q.C., stood up and said, "My Lord, I represent the Sisters of St. Theresa."

"Does the Pope know about this?" the Chief Justice inquired.

Here's a report from Mr. Justice Melvin E. Shannon of the Court of Queen's Bench of Alberta:

"Some years ago, it was the practice in Calgary and Edmonton to set the civil cases down for trial by a procedure known as 'fixing the list.' Counsel were required to attend at the courthouse before a judge on a Friday afternoon ten days before the week in which the case would be heard, to have their cases assessed as to readiness for trial and duration.

"The judge would take them in the order in which they had been entered in the clerk's office and arrange the list of cases to be heard for the week that would commence ten days later. As a result a great number of lawyers would be present in the courtroom, with a judge presiding at this session.

"One day the late Justice Allen Cullen was presiding, and a young Jewish lawyer suggested that his case be heard on the coming Friday, which just happened to be Good Friday. On applying to have his case set for that date, he had overlooked the fact that it was a holiday.

"Mr. Justice Cullen (a devout Roman Catholic) said to him, 'Young man, if we are to proceed on that day, you will have to change your religion or I will have to change mine – and I'm too old for surgery.' "

Duncan Fraser, Q.C., of Brockville, Ontario, recently represented a young woman in a paternity action. He and his opponent asked for a fairly long adjournment so that blood tests could be taken and they could prepare for trial.

"My friend and I suggest December 9th as the date for trial," Fraser told Judge Ross Fair.

"You were wise not to choose December 8th," Judge Fair observed.

"Why, Your Honour?"

"Well, I see by my ecclesiastical calendar that that's the Feast of the Immaculate Conception."

Speaking of conception, court reporter Gail McGilvray of London, Ontario, sent me the following snippet from a recent trial:

COUNSEL: You became pregnant with Jennifer. How did that happen, if you weren't planning it?
MR. JUSTICE JOSEPH POTTS: Well, I think I can take judicial notice of that, having seven children myself.

Robert Del Frate, a lawyer in Sudbury, has a story about a judge who took "judicial notice" of what constitutes a boulder. In a lawsuit Bob was involved in, a contractor testified that his bill for bulldozing was higher than originally estimated because he "ran into unexpected boulders."

"What is your definition of a boulder?" he was asked.

"A rock that I can't move by hand," he replied.

"At my place," observed Judge George E. Collins, "a boulder is a rock that my wife can't move by hand."

Gail McGilvray also sends this snappy excerpt from the cross-examination of a psychiatrist:

Q. Do you have a certificate in a particular specialty?

A. At the completion of the prerequisite training to be a psychiatrist in this country, I wrote and passed the fellowship exams, which at that time was the highest academic standing in the country. Only about two percent of the psychiatrists attained that level. They now give it out like Corn Flakes – it's like a Q.C.

MR. JUSTICE WILLIAM J. ANDERSON: That's a low blow, doctor.

Former Provincial Court Judge S. Tupper Bigelow, Q.C., recalls a case from his days at the bar:

"In a divorce case I had before the late Mr. Justice Keiller Mackay, I called the private detective I had employed to get the evidence on the male defendant. After establishing his purpose and saying how he got into the room, I asked him to describe the room and its contents. He said, 'The defendant, whom I recognized, was clad in a singlet and shorts, and when I knocked at the door and said "Telegram," he opened the door and I went into the room before he could stop me.

"There was an empty bottle of scotch whisky on the bureau and another one about three-quarters full. There were ashtrays on the bureau and on a chair beside the bed, all overflowing. There was men's clothing on a chair and women's clothing on the floor. In the bed, there was a naked lady . . .'

"Said His Lordship, ever the student of precise English, 'A naked *what?*' "

James Thurber began a review of a book about penguins with the observation that "this book tells me a great deal more about penguins than I wanted to know." Mr. Justice George L. Murray of the Supreme Court of British Columbia has a story that Thurber would have enjoyed. It goes as follows:

"Some years ago, a Vancouver lawyer applied to Chief Justice Wilson in chambers for an order to dispense with naming a co-respondent in a divorce case, on the ground that there had been the contraction of a venereal disease. He cited at great length from a reported judgment of Chief Justice E. K. Williams in Manitoba, holding that crabs was a venereal disease.

"At the conclusion of his argument the Chief Justice said, 'I want to thank you for the most useless piece of information I have ever received in my entire career on the bench!' "

Toronto lawyer Robert B. McGee, Q.C., recalls a theft case heard by the late Magistrate C. A. (Gus) Thoburn in the 1960s. The accused had a long record of thievery, and the Crown's case appeared to be overwhelming.

"Can I take the witness box?" asked the alleged culprit.

"You might as well," quipped Thoburn, "you've taken everything else!"

A decade or so ago, a Calgary lawyer told Provincial Court Judge Fred Thurgood that he wished to introduce the results of a polygraph test into evidence at trial.

"What's a polygraph?" Judge Thurgood asked.

"It's a lie detector."

"In this court," His Honour observed, "*I'm* the lie detector."

In Calgary the Provincial Court concludes for the day at four o'clock – on the dot. Indeed, witnesses and lawyers have been shushed in mid-sentence, even mid-word, when the magic time arrives.

Judge Brian C. Stevenson recalls the following exchange between a five-foot-three lawyer and Judge G. G. Cioni:

"I note that it's five minutes to four, Your Honour. I have only one short witness left to testify."

"A relative?"

Back in 1950, when I was sweet sixteen, "Goodnight Irene" was number one on the Hit Parade for ages. You couldn't go anywhere on this planet, it seemed, without hearing that infernal tune blasting out of a jukebox or radio. I recall reading a news story about a man who was shot dead because he failed to heed a warning to stop playing it on the jukebox in a bar.

Mr. Justice Willard Estey of the Supreme Court of Canada takes us back to those days:

"One dark and wintry day in the Supreme Court of Canada, Chief Justice Rinfret, a small Santa Claus-like figure, was presiding over an inordinately dull appeal brought by the musicians, authors, and composers of ASCAP for the recovery of royalties. Their counsel, Mr. Harold Manning, K.C., was a nationally known copyright expert. He had been intoning on the dreary copyright laws of England and Canada and the virtues of his clients for some hours, while the snow fell in the encircling darkness outside. Suddenly Chief Justice Rinfret sat up in his usual spritely fashion and said, 'Mr. Manning, would it be out of order for me to inquire whether your clients' repertoire includes "Goodnight Irene"?' "

I *told* you that judgin' could be pretty dreary at times, didn't I? Lawyers often don't know when to pack it in. Some of them waste a lot of time and repeat themselves a great deal. One lawyer began his cross-examination of a woman by asking her how many children she had, and about an hour later he asked her again. Before she could open her mouth the judge remarked, "When you began, she had three."

In another case, after counsel had been addressing the jury for a long time, repeating himself constantly and not giving the slightest hint that the end was nigh, the judge snapped, "Mr. Smith, you've said that before!"
"Have I, My Lord?" came the reply. "I'm very sorry. I quite forgot it."
"Don't apologize," said the judge. "I forgive you, for it was a long time ago."

Mr. Justice Rodman E. Logan of the Court of Queen's Bench of New Brunswick tells a story about an earlier member of that court, Mr. Justice John Prescott, who responded to the clarion call of supper. Here's the tale:

"Evidence was concluded in a civil case tried in Edmundston, and Jack said to counsel, 'Gentlemen, how long will you be in argument?' Counsel for the plaintiff said he'd be fifteen or twenty minutes. Counsel for the defendant, a rather long-winded, pompous man, said 'Oh, I doubt very much if I can finish in less than an hour.'
"It was late in a winter's afternoon and the lights were on in the courtroom. There was nobody there except the judge, the court reporter, and the lawyers. Jack looked at counsel for the defendant and said, 'That's fine. Turn the lights out when you leave, would you, please?' "

District Court Judge Donald G. E. Thompson of Owen Sound, Ontario, recalls a long-winded lawyer who confessed to the court, "I'm afraid I've been quite redundant."

"You can say that again," the judge replied.

In another case, a lawyer had been getting so many hurry-up signals from the judge that he said to a witness, "Without belabouring the point, please state your name."

London, Ontario, court reporter Gail McGilvray sends this tidbit from a recent trial in the Supreme Court of Ontario:

LAWYER: My Lord, I will guarantee to be two minutes in re-examination. The clerk can give me the hook if I go any longer.

MR. JUSTICE JOHN WHITE: I didn't know he had one, or I would have used it by now myself.

As a court clerk and later as Justice of the Peace, Peter Breen has served for thirty years in one of Canada's busiest courthouses – Old City Hall in Toronto. In those three decades he's been present at thousands of trials and he's heard hundreds of funny remarks from bench and bar. We go back to the early 1960s for his all-time favourite.

Toronto morality detectives had decided to "bust" the Victory Theatre. For some time, the Victory had been showing movies and strippers, in that order, several times a day – at 1:30, 4:30, 7:30, and 10:30, to be precise.

Two detectives dropped in to catch the 4:30 show. Spying pubic hair protruding from the G-string of one of the dancers, they charged the manager with presenting an immoral theatrical performance and the dancer with participating in same.

"The officers are lying!" the stripper told Magistrate Joseph Addison. "They *couldn't* have seen any hair, because there *wasn't* any! I was shaven, Your Worship. All us girls shave."

"Perhaps it was five o'clock shadow," Magistrate Addison suggested.

8

The Entertainers

All work and no play makes Jack a dull boy.

–ANON.

If you cling to the view, as many folks do, that lawyers and judges are all solemn, stuffy bores, then two will get you ten that you haven't heard tell of Dwayne Rowe or Chris Evans or Hal Sisson. In that case, introductions are in order.

At various times during his forty-six years, Dwayne Wade Rowe has been a store clerk, newspaperman, radio personality, television comedy writer, stand-up comic, practising lawyer, Deputy Magistrate in the Yukon, Provincial Court Judge in Alberta, and, since 1985, a Deputy Judge of the Territorial Court of the Yukon. When he's not dispensing justice, Judge Rowe chips away at a screenplay he's writing and dreams up gags and sells them to cartoonists and comedians. His Honour has flogged dozens of one-liners to comedienne Joan Rivers.

Christopher D. Evans, Q.C., of Calgary was a classmate of Rowe's in law school and his partner from 1979 to 1984. Rowe articled with Harold C. Sisson, Q.C., of Peace River, Alberta, in 1963–64 and was his partner for five years after that.

Judge Rowe has warm memories of both his former partners. He affectionately describes Evans as "a well-known columnist, trial lawyer, writer, singer, radio and TV commentator, iconoclast, and nut-case." Sisson, who practised law for thirty-three years until his retirement in 1986, has been known for most of that time as one of Alberta's best actors and comedians. Hal was the driving force behind the establishment of Peace Players, a drama group in Peace River, and for twenty consecutive years he's produced an extremely popular burlesque-vaudeville show called "Sorry 'Bout That."

Rowe had been a Provincial Court Judge for nearly five years – in Grande Prairie, Medicine Hat, and Calgary – when he turned in his judicial robe in 1979 to start a private legal practice in Calgary with his old friend Chris Evans and a younger lawyer named John Bascom. In a feature article published shortly thereafter, Calgary *Herald* writer Bruce Masterman noted: "His absurd sense of humour, coupled with a knowledge of criminal law developed since he was admitted to the Alberta bar in 1964, has made Rowe a legend in the legal community and a thorn in the side of all levels of government. 'The goddamn bureaucrats have too much influence over the system,' Rowe complained during an interview in his sparsely furnished office on the fourth floor of the Lougheed Building."

Knowing that Evans and Rowe were outstanding lawyers, with hordes of well-heeled clients, I wondered about that reference to a "sparsely furnished office." Could it be that these high-priced legal luminaries, two of the best lawyers in Alberta, were a mite miserly in matters of decor? I asked this question of Rowe, and a split-second later he replied, "Oh yes! And why not? After all, you can't eat the gross." Truer words were never spoken.

"You should have seen our waiting room!" His Honour said with great pride. "It was the epitome of bad taste!

"We had two tacky chairs and a beat-up old table – that's all. The whole 'ensemble' cost about sixty dollars. Clients would sit in those ratty old chairs, in the very building where Prime Minister R. B. Bennett used to practise law, and they'd listen to the radiator clank and wile away the time reading the press clippings we had plastered everywhere."

Whenever one of the partners was mentioned in dispatches, the entire article, with the lawyer's name highlighted in yellow, was tacked to a board in the waiting room or taped to one of the walls thereof.

"We had clippings all over the office, not just in the waiting room," Rowe said enthusiastically. "They were stuck to the side of the photocopier, taped on doors, doorjambs, walls, window sills–wherever there was room to put them, up they went! We had no shame!"

That's for sure.

Dominating one wall of the waiting room was a huge poster of an exhausted marathon runner, bent over and throwing up, and underneath was the caption, "Evans in the Court of Appeal." Nearby was a picture of Igor Gouzenko, of spy-trials fame, peering out through the eye-holes of the white hood he wore on all occasions. Beneath Igor was the caption, "Bascom, After Arguing Another Impaired-Driving Case."

The firm of Evans, Rowe and Bascom took on a lot of big cases, in exchange for hefty fees, and Rowe says that when clients strolled into the waiting room for the first time they were always astounded by "the godawful look of the place."

In those days, Chris Evans was a bencher of the Law Society of Alberta – one of the small group of practitioners who, in effect, run the profession throughout the province – and Rowe often represented the law society at disciplinary hearings. "Benchers and other lawyers would often come to our office to conduct law-society business," Rowe said, "and they'd be absolutely horrified at our complete lack of good taste."

One day, shortly after one of these visits, Chris Evans found a way to further impair the firm's image in the eyes of the law society. In the process, he demonstrated why one magazine writer referred to him as "establishment needler-at-large."

An unknown man had been sexually assaulting women in the southwest section of Calgary, and nearly every day for several months the media had reported on the search for "the Southwest Rapist." At the height of the manhunt, Evans came across a large photograph, in living colour, of the benchers of the Law Society of Alberta. He promptly scribbled a caption and tacked the new production on a waiting-room wall. The caption read: "One of These Men is Probably the Southwest Rapist."

In 1979 the firm undertook the defence of a man charged with defrauding a company of $1.2 million through a series of extremely complicated transactions said to have taken place in Bermuda, South Africa, Switzerland, Vancouver, and many other locations. After a five-week preliminary hearing and a six-week jury trial, the accused was acquitted. But that was all "down the road," and no one could possibly have known at the outset that there'd be a happy ending.

On the first day of court the accused and his wife sat squirming in that incredible waiting room, pending the arrival of Christopher D. Evans, Q.C., who was sponging himself down after his morning run. The lady had never been in the office before, nor had she ever met the lawyers who'd be trying to save her husband from a long stretch in prison. As she scanned the clippings and "art work" on the walls, she must have wondered why they'd entrusted such a grave matter to men who were obviously kooks. What she saw and heard in the next few minutes didn't make her feel any better.

Chris Evans shuffled into the waiting room in floppy slippers and a bathrobe. In one of his hands he clutched a rubber duck. The man beside him, Dwayne Rowe, was decked out in a nifty pin-striped suit –

"the Calgary lawyer's home uniform," Rowe calls it – and he held a smart-looking attaché case packed with papers and books that would be needed in court.

Evans squeezed the duck a couple of times, then said to the woman, "Hello, I'm Chris Evans and this is my partner, Mr. Rowe. Now don't worry, ma'am. Your husband's life is in our hands. I'll be right back."

In short order, Evans was back in the waiting room, resplendent in a pin-striped uniform and carrying an attaché case that was ready for action. The four then left the office.

As they headed toward the elevator, Evans decided that some cheering-up was in order. He suddenly grabbed Rowe's hand and they skipped down the hallway, swinging their briefcases and singing, "Hi ho, hi ho, it's off to court we go!"

Maybe the lady was right. Maybe these fellows *are* kooks.

Well, I dunno. Another way of looking at it – the right way, I think – is that they're a couple of hardworking, irrepressible blokes who are blessed with the ability to extinguish tension at will and instantly refresh themselves with some good old-fashioned fun. It's a gift – a rare gift.

Dwayne Rowe and Chris Evans have been horsing around together since law-school days. When they were partners, there were lots of laughs around the office – moments of merriment that sprang up suddenly and left everyone re-energized and happy to get back to work. Like the time a rookie policeman came to the office to give Rowe a parking ticket.

Rowe was in the reception room when the officer arrived.

"Excuse me," the officer said to one of the secretaries, "I'm looking for a Mr. Dwayne Rowe." He was holding a small piece of paper in his hand.

Rowe turned on his heels, sprinted into his office, locked the door and screamed: "I'm not going back to the Big House! You'll never take me alive, copper!"

The police officer, a chap who'd seen perhaps nineteen summers, anxiously approached the door to communicate with the fugitive from justice.

"Mr. Rowe," he said through the door, "it's only a five-dollar ticket."

"Get lost, flatfoot!" screamed the man within. "I'm never going back! Do you *hear* me? *Never! Never!*"

The officer slid the ticket under the door and left the premises forthwith.

"Chris and I did a lot of work for the Calgary Police Association, defending members when they got into trouble," Rowe said. "The young officer went back and reported to the brass in the association that they were dealing with a couple of lunatics. Of course, he was correct."

Who knows, if Evans and Rowe hadn't chosen the life of the law they might have ended up on the silver screen. Many a legal gathering has wildly cheered the capers of these masters of mirth. They work together as smoothly as Abbott and Costello or Laurel and Hardy. The larger the crowd, the more they throw themselves into their outrageous skits, "stand-up" routines, and impressions. Once, in Dawson City, they wowed a crowd of two thousand conventioneering Kinsmen. On another occasion, they whipped up a slightly smaller assembly on the sidewalks of New York . . .

As part of the preliminary inquiry in the aforementioned million-dollar fraud case, Rowe and Evans travelled to Bermuda to examine under oath a large number of top executives of South African companies alleged to be involved in a complex swindle. These men weren't willing to travel to Canada to testify, but they did agree to be grilled in Bermuda. On their way to the inquisition, defence counsel paid a brief but memorable visit to Manhattan.

Returning to their hotel, the boys suddenly decided to put on a show for the throngs of people who were still streaming through Times Square at two in the morning. Like a couple of vaudevillians, they danced around and carried on a line of patter until they'd brought a few hundred pedestrians to a halt. Then, as the crowd of onlookers continued to grow, Chris Evans broke loose.

Swinging around a lamp post like Gene Kelly, he shouted to Rowe, "If I could just finish this song that's been playing around in my head since we left the farm."

"How does it go, Clem?" yelled Rowe.

"It goes like this . . ." Evans danced around the lamp post, warbling "Singing in the – "

He stopped, then danced up and down the front steps of a nearby building, glided gracefully back to the lamp post, twirled around the post several times and tried again: "Singing in the –"

Undaunted, Chris continued to trip the light fantastic – up the steps, down the steps, back to the post, twirling and whirling. "Singing in the –"

Finally, somebody bit. From the back of the crowd came the dulcet tones of a voice born in Brooklyn: "Rain, for fuck sake! Rain!"

A short time later, Evans and Rowe set up shop in Bermuda and returned to the un-funny business of trying to save their client from a long term in the pen. Right off the bat, though, the incorrigible quipster Rowe had a relapse. As soon as the first South African witness had been sworn in, he asked: "Apartheid from the plane ride, how did you like your trip?"

"Incorrigible" is the word for Dwayne Rowe. Consider the following, from a feature story on Rowe in the Calgary *Herald*:

"The stern-faced lecturer marched into the University of Alberta law classroom, pointed at a lanky, tousled-haired first-year student and demanded 'an example of assault and battery.'

" 'Sifto and Autolite,' came the instant reply, sparking an explosion of laughter from students and professor alike, and establishing Dwayne Wade Rowe as the clown of the class."

Rowe has a great "feel" for words and the subtleties and nuances of the English language. These attributes, combined with his keen sense of humour, have come in handy whenever he's yielded to the temptation to poke fun at governments and bureaucracy. His early mentor and partner, Hal Sisson, recalls that Rowe would make up fictitious names of "new" companies and send them to the provincial government's companies branch for approval. If they weren't approved, Rowe demanded to know the reason. One of the make-believe companies that officials didn't twig to was a recreational firm called "Sonza Beaches, Ltd."

A few years ago, Rowe, provoked by a statement made by a cabinet minister, fired off this letter to the Calgary *Herald*:

"Dave King, minister of education, is absolutely correct in harbouring the suspicion that sexual education tends to increase sexual activity. In my case, personal experience as a youth corroborates King's fears.

"Upon taking driving education, I drove and drove and drove. Upon learning rudiments of grammar, I would, at the slightest invitation, conjugate in public, shamelessly, with dangling participles fully exposed.

"Basic mathematics compelled me in a frenzy to examine my square root and to toy for hours with integrals, powers and, tawdry as it must seem in print, to fool around with reciprocals.

"Fortunately, a timely visit to an optometrist convinced me to stop. However, it had gone far enough to require being fitted with corrective lenses.

"Sexual potential, like any other storehouse of our Alberta Heritage, must be saved, counted, talked about, but never, God forbid, spent."

During his six years with Hal Sisson in Peace River, Rowe served on town council (1965–68), ran unsuccessfully for Parliament (1968), became exceptionally adept at criminal law, started and ended a radio career, and performed hilariously in the first two annual productions of Sisson's burlesque-vaudeville show, "Sorry 'Bout That." As a matter of fact, that title, from Maxwell Smart's famous TV line, "Sorry about that, chief," was suggested by Rowe. In 1974, when he was a judge in Grande Prairie, Rowe returned to the show and was a smash hit in several skits, especially one called "Dwayne Rowe Rides Again." In the show's 1974 program His Honour is billed as "stand-up comic Dwayne Rowe," and in publicity blurbs he was touted as the "special guest star from the big city."

The versatile Rowe made his radio debut in 1966 on a weekly radio show in Peace River. The show, called "Checkpoint," featured Rowe, an Anglican bishop, a staff announcer, and a high-school teacher discussing local, provincial, and national issues. "I think we had the worst ratings of any program in the history of mankind," Rowe said. "We were sponsored by a local feed store, and before long the sponsor withdrew." Still, you might say, it was good grist for Rowe's mill.

From 1969 to 1971, when he was practising law in Edmonton, Rowe contributed comedy-skit material to two ill-fated CBC television shows – "Comedy Crackers" and "Zut." Writing under the nom de plume of "Gimpy Cleever," Rowe's favourite gags took the form of phony newscasts – still considered by many of his fans to be his forte.

While Rowe's reputation as a comedian continued to grow, so did his renown as an outstanding criminal lawyer. In a 1979 interview, former partner Hal Sisson ranked Rowe "among the top ten criminal lawyers in Canada, perhaps the best in Alberta.

"He has an instinct that helps him go to the legal core of the issues in the courtroom, picking out the weaknesses in the Crown's case," Sisson said. "Instead of a shotgun approach, Rowe uses a rifle and goes straight to the point."

Sisson said that in addition to having a keen legal mind, Rowe was an excellent courtroom showman, a good public speaker, and had "a good sense of theatrics." That description was echoed by former partner and comedy-sidekick Chris Evans, who added that "Dwayne has compassion." Grande Prairie lawyer Jim Watson remembers Rowe as a better-than-average judge who could be "stern and severe" but whose courtroom was seldom completely solemn. "He was a tough sentencer,"

Watson said, "and he had very little trouble making up his mind." When it comes to humour, Watson adds, "He's funnier sober than anyone could be after a few drinks."

Rowe's keen interest in, and knowledge of, show business has occasionally helped him in court. Once, after leaving the bench in the late 1970s, he represented a man who was charged with having "care and control" of his car while impaired by alcohol. The accused had consumed a prodigious amount of booze in a Calgary bar and had then gone to his car in the parking lot. It was thirty degrees below zero at the time.

The man started up his car and, while it was idling, he fell asleep behind the wheel. A short time later, the car caught fire. A passer-by called police and they came on the double. The man had locked the door upon entering the car, and the police had to use special equipment to pry it open. They dragged him out of the vehicle while it was still burning. The car was totally destroyed. Down at the station, the previous occupant's breath practically knocked the breathalyzer machine out of commission.

Rowe pleaded his client guilty before Judge Fred Thurgood, a veteran jurist who's said many a humorous thing in court himself. Rowe relates the rest of the story:

"Judge Thurgood looked at me and said, 'But how on earth did he get inside that burning vehicle?' I replied, 'Well, Your Honour, in order to make an explanation, I'll have to relate to you a story about what happened to a comedian by the name of Stuttering Joe Frisco in the late 1930s.

" 'All right,' Judge Thurgood said. 'Proceed.'

" 'Joe Frisco was an inveterate horse-player, comic, and drinker, and one day the police attended a fire at Frisco's place in Malibu Canyon. When the fire department arrived, the house was in great conflagration and they found Stuttering Joe Frisco lying on a bed in the middle of the living room. They rescued him, and then the fire chief, who knew Joe as a man-about-town, asked him, "How did the fire start?" and Joe replied, "I d-d-d-on't k-k-now, C-hief, it was g-g-g-oing when I w-w-went to b-b-b-ed." '

"Judge Thurgood said, 'It makes sense to me, counsel,' and imposed a very, very light fine under the circumstances."

To Hal Sisson, the man who helped launch Rowe's legal and comedic careers, life without laughter would be unbearable. "Laughter," he says, "is the clinking of a couple of unexpected coins in the shabby pocket of life."

Hal practised law in the small northern Alberta town of Peace River from 1953 until his retirement in 1986. "Law is a serious business," he noted recently, "and what I remember most about the small-town and district practice of law are the times when I had fun and games."

Like the time he and Rowe pulled "the great Diefenbaker caper." One day, during a federal election campaign in the 1960s, Sisson and Rowe, both staunch Conservatives, came across an enormous picture of John Diefenbaker. They took it across the street to the law office of Henry Maddison, secretary of the Liberal Party of Alberta, and persuaded the janitor to let them place it behind the drapes in Maddison's private office. A few days later, the leader of the Liberal Party of Alberta was in Maddison's office, discussing the upcoming election. As he was leaving, he asked the location of a certain hotel. Maddison said, "Look, I'll show you. It's right out the window here." Maddison pulled the drape-cords and out "jumped" John to startle two of his foes.

"It's said that "the Mounties always get their man." But one wonders whether that motto says it all. In 1974 the RCMP marked its centennial, and as part of the national celebrations, the famous RCMP Musical Ride visited Peace River. Thousands of people attended the festivities, including many former residents of the area.

The morning after the performance, Hal Sisson, Q.C., was called to Provincial Court to represent a woman who was a member of a well-known local family. She had returned for the celebrations, had celebrated too enthusiastically, and now found herself charged with causing a disturbance.

Conferring quickly with the Crown Prosecutor, Sisson learned that the woman had appeared in the lobby of a local hotel about four o'clock that morning, wailing and shouting drunkenly. The prosecutor advised that, "in the circumstances," he'd be seeking the minimum penalty.

The "circumstances," as related to the court, were that after the performance the previous afternoon, the woman visited the hotel lounge and there consumed alcoholic beverages with various members of the Musical Ride until after closing. Then . . . well, let's hear how Hal put it:

"Your Honour, after the lounge closed my client went up to a hotel room with several members of the RCMP, and there the Musical Ride continued."

For the first dozen or so years that Sisson was in town, Peace River was lukewarm about having a theatre group. "We didn't have a town idiot in those days," Hal says, "and everyone had to take turns. If you thought it was your turn, you reported to the town office."

In 1967 Sisson must have thought it was his turn. He renewed his previously unsuccessful efforts to organize an amateur theatrical society, and that year – as a Canadian centennial project – Peace Players first saw the light of day.

Sisson had performed in burlesque comedy revues in the wartime RCAF and later at the University of Saskatchewan, and he knew that that type of show would be popular with adult audiences – especially if done in cabaret style. "Sorry 'Bout That" was the group's first production. Based on material that Hal has gathered on trips to Las Vegas, New York, Los Angeles, and London, the show has been packing 'em in for several weekends each year for two decades now. The profits have been ploughed into the construction of a town swimming pool, town tennis courts, renovations to buildings, and many other worthwhile projects.

Peace Players ran the first subscription-series theatre in rural Alberta, bringing a great many touring companies and performers into Peace River to present musicals and plays. "We tried to bring in Racquel Welch to play in "The Hunchfront of Notre Dame," Sisson quips in one issue of the troupe's program, "but she left us flat and holding a bag." In another issue, an admirer writes: "The number of hours that Hal has spent over the years collecting material for our shows, and acting in them, is astronomical. I have heard it said that to be a good lawyer you must be an actor as well. In Hal we can see that this is true. A 'ham' till the end, a great wit, boundless energy and a love of the theatre make up Hal Sisson."

Sisson hung up his lawyer's gown in 1986 – and promptly launched a one-man burlesque comedy show. "Although things may be desperate, they are never serious," Hal proclaimed in promotional material for his new venture, a one-hour, risqué monologue called "Jacques Strapp's Last Crepe." In this production, which was seen and heard every night for a week in an Edmonton hotel, Sisson played an ancient actor reminiscing in an old, closed-down theatre. Audiences loved it. "Rude, crude, and enjoyable," one critic observed.

"Old actors never die – their parts just grow smaller," sixty-six-year-old Hal Sisson remarked recently. He calls himself "a retired and re-formed lawyer" these days. Retired from law, perhaps, but certainly not from life. Hal recently completed a novel, then left for a tour of the Orient. There's lots more writing ahead of him and, of course, show biz never stops beckoning.

And what's this nonsense about Sisson being "reformed?" Please, Hal, don't reform. We *need* hams like you in this vale of tears. You could help a lot of people shake the blues. Why, you might even get together again with your former partner, Judge Dwayne Rowe, and crack off a few gags for TV. It'd be just like old times!

Rowe's hooked, too, you know, and don't forget, you helped make him that way! Remember those one-liners he's sold to Joan Rivers. Here, let me show you a few . . .

- "Edgar and I have personal-touch banking. Our relatives come over at night and borrow money."
- "Celebrity answering-machine: 'Hello, this is George Burns. I'm out at the moment, but I've forgotten where. If I make it back, I'll call you.' "
- "Celebrity answering machine: 'Hi, I'm Dom Deluise. I'm out at the moment, devouring a buffalo. Please leave a message at the sound of the burp.' "
- "Melissa's friend Bambi thinks *First Blood* is a hygiene film."
- "My gynecologist won't cash my cheque without proper I.U.D."
- "Until he invented a bleach for pubic hair, whoever heard of Bruce Boxleitner?"
- "If you throw up on a McDonald's parking lot, do they subtract a number?"
- "Lost your traveller's cheques? Maybe they're in Karl Malden's nose."

I have a lot more here, Hal, but you get the idea. Give Dwayne a call. The poor man needs help.

9

The Case of the Blue Tick Hound

Why shouldn't truth be stranger than fiction?
Fiction, after all, has to make sense.

−MARK TWAIN

This is a true story – absolutely true. Please bear this in mind at all times.

Midland, Ontario, is a pretty town of some twelve thousand souls, situated on Georgian Bay, about a hundred miles northwest of Toronto. The area is steeped in history. The seventeenth-century explorers Brûlé, Champlain, and LaSalle knew it well. So did the Jesuits. They established a mission there in 1639, a courageous venture that ended in tragedy a few years later when six of the good Fathers were burned at the stake.

What Douglas G. Haig went through, three centuries later, can hardly compare with *that*. Still, he must have felt like a bit of a martyr and, like the missionaries, he must have wondered what the hell was going on.

In 1958 young Doug Haig had been practising law in Midland for four years. One morning, in the winter of that year, he and a client strolled from his office to the nondescript hall where Small Claims Court – then called Division Court – was about to start. They were certainly in the right place: Doug's client had launched an action for damages to his car in the princely amount of eighty-nine dollars. The case would be heard by Judge James Gray Harvie, a small, dapper man who was County Court Judge for the County of Simcoe. He was also responsible for deciding disputes in several Division Courts within the county.

Everyone seemed to agree that Judge Harvie was an excellent jurist, but he had a couple of idiosyncrasies. He was almost fanatical in his insistence that everyone in court conduct themselves with the utmost dignity and decorum and, as we've seen in an earlier chapter, he usually brought his tiny chihuahua dog into court with him. The dog was so small it fit into its master's vest pocket. That's where it was the day Doug Haig and his client went to court to fight for eighty-nine dollars.

Court started promptly at ten in the morning. His Honour zipped through a few routine matters, then plunged into the main business at hand. Doug Haig was pleased that his case was second on the trial list. "We should be out of here fairly soon," he told his client as the first case got underway.

The first case was Desroches versus Murphy, a dispute over the ownership of a big Blue Tick Hound. The plaintiff, his wife, and eight of their children testified that the family had once owned a Blue Tick Hound whose name was Pierre. They all said it was a wonderful pet and a good guard dog.

Mr. Desroches and his two eldest sons said in their testimony that Pierre was a great hunting dog, too. With Pierre accompanying them, they said, they'd hunted deer, rabbits, and foxes with great success. They described the dog in minute detail. They'd bought it as a puppy several years before its disappearance, they said, and the hound had vanished on them a few years before the start of the court proceedings.

In his testimony, Mr. Desroches said that about a year after his dog had disappeared, he was driving through nearby Victoria Harbour when, lo and behold, there was his dog, walking along the street. He said he stopped immediately, called the dog over, put him in the car and drove a few blocks to a detachment of the Ontario Provincial Police. There, he said, he reported that he had found his long-lost Blue Tick Hound, gave his name and address, and then left with the dog.

The plaintiff and his family had an excellent reputation in the district around Lafontaine, a French community about ten miles west of Midland, and they called several character witnesses to attest to this. When it came to truthfulness, the witnesses all agreed, the Desroches family was tops.

At the end of the plaintiff's case, the defendant Murphy and his wife and numerous children testified that they lived in Victoria Harbour, about ten miles east of Midland, and several years before the court case they'd bought a mature Blue Tick Hound from friends in Orillia. They said their dog couldn't hunt – in fact, he was gun-shy – but they adored the big, lovable rascal they called "Blue."

Mr. Murphy stated that a few days after his dog had disappeared, he went to the OPP detachment at Victoria Harbour and reported the matter to the officer in charge. He was told that Mr. Desroches, from

Lafontaine, had picked up a dog similar to the one he'd just described. Murphy went to the Desroches residence, saw his dog, and asked to have it returned to him. Mr. Desroches refused, and Murphy left in a huff. He returned a few days later and "dognapped" the Blue Tick Hound.

Every member of the Murphy family testified that the dog they'd purchased and the dog they'd liberated were one and the same dog. They were positive of this. And yet it was clear that one dog could not be *both* the dog owned by the Desroches family and the dog owned by the Murphys.

It was now one o'clock in the afternoon. Court was adjourned till two. Judge Harvie said he'd consider the dilemma over the lunch hour, and he suggested that in the meantime it might be helpful if the Murphys drove to Victoria Harbour, fetched the dog, and brought it to court.

Doug Haig's client wondered when his case would be heard. Haig said, "shortly after lunch," and assured him that his twenty-dollar fee would not be increased one cent because of the delay.

When court reopened at two o'clock, Judge Harvie directed the clerk to sit the dog in the centre of the courtroom between the two counsel – A. B. Thompson of Penetanguishene, who acted for the plaintiff Desroches, and Oliver H. Smith, Q.C., of Midland, who appeared for the defendant Murphy. The judge's chihuahua peeked out of one of its master's vest pockets, its itty-bitty eyes peering around the courtroom and coming to rest, nervously, on the beefy Blue Tick Hound that sat close by.

Judge Harvie asked each of the witnesses who'd testified in the morning to come up and look at the dog and state under oath whether or not it was that person's dog and, if it was, to explain how he or she knew that to be so.

"One after another," Doug Haig recalls, "both sets of parents and all of the children from both families dutifully came forward and swore that the dog was their family dog, some of the younger children breaking into tears. It was obvious from the look on His Honour's face that he was completely perplexed. Then he had a sudden inspiration that proved to be disastrous."

Remembering that the Desroches family called their dog Pierre, Judge Harvie, the man who was so hell-bent on courtroom decorum, decided to play a game. He told the clerk, "Now, you have the dog sit quietly in the centre there, and I'll call him by name and we'll see if he comes."

"Come, Pierre!" shouted the judge.

The big Blue Tick Hound raised himself from his haunches and leaped across the courtroom, up the steps onto the dais, and into the lap of Judge Harvie. In the excitement, the startled chihuahua dived to the bottom of the judge's vest pocket.

Judge Harvie's great dignity never left him for a moment. He simply told the clerk to come and get the hound and return him to the body of the courtroom. When this had been done, Doug Haig couldn't help noticing a large wet spot on the lower part of His Honour's vest.

The dog had responded swiftly and unequivocally to "Pierre." To the judge's way of thinking, that pretty well determined the issue. He had started to say that the verdict would go to Desroches when Oliver Smith, the lawyer for Murphy, rose to his feet and said, "With all due respect, Your Honour, in order for the test to be fair and complete, you should call the dog again, this time using the name that my client and his family have always used for their dog. That name, as you have heard, is 'Blue.' "

Judge Harvie said Smith's submission made some sense. Once again, he directed the clerk to position the dog in the centre of the courtroom.

"Come, Blue!" boomed the judge.

In a second or two, the speedy hound was back in the judge's lap and the chihuahua had taken refuge in the deepest part of the vest pocket. The clerk hauled the dog off His Honour.

"Court will recess for a few minutes," a frustrated Judge Harvie announced. As he rose to leave, the chihuahua's tiny head popped back into view. Doug Haig noted that the wet spot on the vest was twice as big as before.

A few minutes later, the clerk returned to the court and said that the judge would see counsel in his office. "He wants you to come in, too," the clerk told Haig. "I wonder why," Doug remarked.

The three lawyers trooped in to see the judge. "By this time His Honour had sponged himself quite adequately," Haig says, "and he was determined to have the matter resolved."

"There's a complete conflict in the evidence," Judge Harvie told the lawyers, as if they didn't know. "But I see a possible way out of this," he added hopefully.

"What's that, Your Honour?" someone asked.

"The Desroches family testified that their dog was a great hunter, and the Murphys said that the dog they had couldn't hunt worth a damn and was gun-shy. That's the only aspect of this dilemma that offers any hope of solution."

The lawyers wondered what he was driving at.

"Mr. Haig," the judge said, "you've been in court all day, you've heard all the evidence. There's something I want you to do – as a friend of the court."

"What's that, Your Honour?"

"They tell me you're a good hunter."

"Well, yes, I . . . I am."

"I want you to take this dog out into the bush, as soon as possible, and find out whether or not he's a good hunter, and whether or not he's gun-shy. I need this information to help me decide the case."

Doug Haig thought for a moment, then said he'd conduct such a field trial on condition that the lawyers for the parties come along with him. Both lawyers agreed, and the safari was set for the following Saturday morning.

Back in court, Judge Harvie told the parties and the hordes of witnesses that Mr. Douglas Haig, local lawyer and hunting authority, had kindly consented to conduct a field trial, the object of which was to determine whether the hound was or was not a hunter by nature. He added that the lawyers involved in the case would accompany Mr. Haig into the wilderness and assist him in any way they could.

"Now, Mr. Haig," the judge said in court, "you are to report directly to me at the beginning of the week. I will then decide the case."

"Do we go on now?" Haig's anxious client inquired.

"I'm afraid not," Doug said. "It's well after four o'clock, and the judge has to get back to Barrie. Besides, he probably wants to change his clothes."

Judge Harvie adjourned court for a month, then strode out of the courtroom – rather quickly, Haig noted – and headed for his car. The eighty-nine-dollar case would have to wait till next time.

On Saturday morning Doug Haig called the plaintiff's lawyer and learned, from the lawyer's wife, that he'd been partying the night before and was in no condition to go traipsing around in the bush. As a matter of fact, she said, he'd refused to get out of bed to answer the phone.

Haig then called the defendant's lawyer. Ditto. The fellow was in rough shape and couldn't possibly attend the field trial. Sorry. Some other time, perhaps.

What to do?

"I made a foolish decision," Doug said recently. "I decided to go ahead with the field trial without them."

Haig drove to the Murphy residence in Victoria Harbour, picked up the Blue Tick Hound, and drove ten miles to a swamp he knew was filled with rabbits and foxes.

"The hound was very friendly," he recalls. "He sat in the front seat and kept licking my ear all the way out.

"When we got to the swamp and I took him into the bush, he gambolled about and had a great time chasing chickadees and other winter birds. He paid no attention to any of the rabbit tracks that were criss-crossing his trail in all directions. At one point he even missed a rabbit that darted off within a few feet of his nose. He looked at the rabbit, followed it for thirty or forty feet, and then gave up.

"I quickly came to the conclusion that Blue was not a good hunter. But to fully determine the matter for His Honour, I had to see if the dog was gun-shy. I waited till he was a reasonable distance from me, then I pointed my 12-gauge shotgun in the air and discharged it. Immediately, a blue streak whizzed through the cedar swamp in the general direction of York County. I spent most of the rest of the day crashing about in the swamp, yelling 'Here Blue!' and 'Here Pierre!' with no results whatsoever."

Just before dark, Doug Haig decided he'd had enough. He returned to his car, hoping the hound would be there, but there was no sign of him anywhere in the vicinity.

"I drove around the whole concession block surrounding the swamp, but the dog was nowhere to be seen," Haig said. "I spoke to several people I met, but they hadn't seen the dog. Finally, I drove back to Victoria Harbour and reported to the Murphy family that I'd conducted the field trial and was satisfied I had enough information to report to the judge. I had to admit to them, however, that the dog had disappeared."

On Monday morning, the concientious young lawyer called Judge Harvie and told him everything that had happened the previous Saturday.

"You've done a great job, Doug," the judge said. "I know what to do now."

"But, Your Honour, the dog got away! He's vanished!"

"Don't worry, my boy. I didn't like that damn hound anyway."

Several weeks later, Judge Harvie brought down his judgment. As a result of the excellent field trial conducted by Douglas Haig as "friend of the court," His Honour declared that this was one Blue Tick Hound that wasn't a good hunting dog. Therefore, he'd concluded, the dog belonged to the Murphys. Blue would be back home with them – if and when he was found.

"I have always been satisfied that justice was done," says Douglas G. Haig, Q.C., "and I have never since volunteered to be a 'friend of the court' or to conduct any field trials."

The eighty-nine-dollar case that had brought Haig to court in the first place was tried a month later.

"How'd you do?" I asked.

"I can't even remember," Doug confessed.

As far as anyone knows, the Blue Tick Hound is still running. If he is, he wouldn't be much bigger than Judge Harvie's chihuahua by now.

10

The Polish Prince

Al Wachowich isn't a doctor, but that doesn't stop him from handing out prescriptions. His favourite, the one that governs his own life, reads as follows: "The best medicine is a good belly laugh."

Work hard, help others, and, for God's sake, have some fun – that's the philosophy of life of His Lordship, Allan Harvey Joseph Wachowich, Justice of the Court of Queen's Bench of Alberta.

Mr. Justice Wachowich doesn't go looking for humour, the way most folks do. It seems to pop up all around him, begging for recognition. "I find so much of it in everyday situations," he says, "and it provides that zest for life that keeps one going."

Like the time a chap named Lubkiwski was charged with assault with a weapon, an offence that carries a maximum sentence of ten years in prison. What, pray tell, is funny about *that*? Nothing, except that the alleged weapon was a garbage can the accused hurled at another fellow. "Only a Polish judge would understand how a garbage can might be an offensive weapon," Mr. Justice Wachowich said after ruling that in this case it wasn't.

His Lordship is proud of his Polish ancestry, and his talk, on and off the bench, is peppered with references to it. "I learned at an early age that one of the best ways to tell a joke is to tell jokes about one's self," he says. "If you can laugh at yourself, other people will laugh *with* you. You shouldn't feel too sensitive about what they say about you unless they're being cruel, and usually they're not."

That's why, back in university days, young Al Wachowich dubbed himself "The Polish Prince." For more than thirty years, the moniker has stuck.

"Al Wachowich is a unique and refreshing character," says one of his best friends, Edmonton sportscaster Al McCann. "He's dead serious about his work, but he refuses to slip into that mould of stuffy judge. He's no clone. He loves to have fun."

Though much of the fun takes place outside the courtroom, Mr. Justice Wachowich is not averse to injecting some spontaneous humour into the proceedings. In a motor-vehicle case a woman testified that the accident happened because the male driver of the other car made "a quickie turn" into a motel. "No doubt the accident resulted in the slowing down of the 'quickie,' " His Lordship noted.

In an attempted-rape case based largely on circumstantial evidence, Mr. Justice Wachowich chided the prosecutor for his choice of words in summing up the case for the Crown. "In a case of this nature," he teased, "I don't think it's appropriate for you to refer to 'little snatches of evidence.' "

Lawyer Karen Bang represented a bank in a lawsuit heard by Wachowich. After hearing argument for both sides, the judge made up his mind quickly and, just as swiftly, delivered the verdict: "Bang, you're dead!"

"Know thy judge" is an expression lawyers often use in stressing the importance of appreciating the idiosyncrasies of the person who'll hear and decide a case. "Know thy lawyer" is important, too, especially if you're a judge who avoids giving unnecessary offence. In a case heard a few years ago, Mr. Justice Wachowich chose an unorthodox way of telling a lawyer he'd lost. "I knew he wouldn't mind," His Lordship says.

The case was Taylor versus Pacific Petroleums Ltd. After eight days of trial, followed by the writing and signing of a forty-two-page judgment, the judge thought the best way to advise the lawyer of his defeat was to send him a telegram. It read: "Flash! Sell all shares in Pacific Petroleums before noon today. Wachowich."

The recipient of that wire knew exactly what the sender meant, but the lawyer in the next story didn't have the foggiest idea of what was going on. One summer, when the Wachowichs were at their cottage, a colleague, Mr. Justice Michael O'Byrne, had a place nearby. O'Byrne went on a trip for a few days and left his two Irish setters, Fogarty and Brighty, in the care of his twin sons. The sons let the dogs out and they didn't return. All night long, vacationers were kept awake by the youngsters yelling, "Here Fogarty! Here Brighty!" over and over again. Eventually, they found Brighty. But Fogarty vanished forever.

Two years later, at the start of a drug case, the prosecutor bowed to the judge and said, "Good morning, Your Lordship, my name is Fogarty."

"Oh, good," said Mr. Justice Wachowich, "they've found O'Byrne's dog!"

The January 9, 1981, issue of the Edmonton *Journal* contained the following dispatch from a war-torn front:

"As he pulled into his driveway after a restful Christmas holiday with relatives, Al McCann observed a rusty Cadillac adorning his lawn. No ordinary Caddy, either. As he inched closer, he discovered the once-distinguished powder-blue 1967 model was fully equipped except for a motor and front wheels.

"The Wachowich-McCann feud was on again.

"So, with television viewers as witnesses, the CFRN sportscaster retaliated. Following his 6:30 P.M. Thursday sportscast, he gleefully unveiled a large framed colour photograph depicting the usually dignified Court of Queen's Bench Justice Allan Wachowich, chest bared, peering seductively from beneath the bedcovers.

"It was, declared Mr. McCann solemnly, to be bequeathed to the provincial courthouse to be displayed in a suitable area.

"Justice Wachowich was less than overwhelmed and a trifle miffed by the gift. 'I didn't think he would use the media,' the judge weakly protested later. 'I think he's taking unfair advantage of his position.' Besides, he said, it's Mr. McCann's birthday on Friday, 'and I like to buy Caddies for my friends on their birthdays. I find it very fulfilling.'

"The friendly game of one-upmanship began thirteen years ago when Justice Wachowich presented the McCanns with a live goose. Mr. McCann acknowledged the gift with a live raccoon.

"The annual Christmas contest continued until 1979, when a one-year truce was called because the McCanns went south for Christmas.

"He's saying I'm in contempt of court for this one,' laughed Mr. McCann Thursday evening. 'I still think my last gift was best.'

"Followers of the Wachowich-McCann game will recall the Christmas, 1979, occasion when Mr. McCann erected a sign outside Justice Wachowich's home proclaiming: 'Rich Judge Has Free Drinks For Polish Catholics' – which friends and strangers sought to take advantage of.

"As for the Caddy that Justice Wachowich got for a good price from an auto-parts dealer – the price of towing – Mr. McCann has reconsidered his original decision to have it towed back to the judge's lawn. He's now willing to sell. Any offers?"

"This nonsense with McCann is a good outlet for me," said the jurist, who normally deals with very weighty matters. "We see fun everywhere."

I wondered who was "leading" in the twenty-year "war" of pranks.

"Wachowich says he's ahead, but I say *I'm* ahead," McCann replied. "No one really knows, and no one really cares. I'll tell you one thing, though."

"What's that?"

"I really got him with the Christmas trees."

"What's this about Christmas trees?"

"Oh, I thought you knew. Okay, here's the story."

One yuletide, McCann was talking to a couple of fellows who were selling Christmas trees. They told him they'd overstocked and, come the big day, they expected to have a helluva lot of trees left over that they'd have to take to the dump.

"I have just the place for them," McCann said. "I'll gladly take them off your hands."

"Great!" the men said in unison.

"But you'll have to transport them for me."

"No problem."

A few days later, while the Wachowichs were enjoying a skiing vacation, two large trucks crammed with Christmas trees rumbled up their driveway. For the next two or three hours, McCann and his helpers positioned a couple of hundred trees everywhere they could on the Wachowich property – on the big front lawn, in the big backyard, on the swimming pool, on the verandah, up against the hedge – and then they planted signs that said "Judge Wachowich Offering Christmas Trees, Cheap" and "Polish Judge Special on Christmas Trees."

When the Wachowichs returned home, they couldn't believe their eyes. "It was like a forest, everywhere," said His Lordship, who had to pay to have three trucks take the evidence to the dump. "No doubt about it, McCann won that round."

McCann and Wachowich called a ceasefire a couple of years ago. "But you never know," McCann says. "It could start up again at any time – whenever one of us gets a good idea."

Mr. Justice Wachowich concurs. "I'm lying in the weeds," he says, "just waiting for McCann to raise his head."

"Wachowich is a tough judge, but he cares a great deal about people," says one of his colleagues, who prefers to remain anonymous. "He can identify with the underdog because, for most of his life, he's been an underdog. You know, when I think of it, Al's done bloody well for himself."

His Lordship's grandparents left Poland in the late 1890s. After short stays in North Dakota and Manitoba they established a homestead in the wilderness, where the northern Alberta community of Skaro stands today. Allan's parents, Philip and Nancy, had six daughters and two sons. Allan, the seventh child, was born at Opal, Alberta (population "about forty-six," he says), and he had his first few years of schooling there before the family moved to Edmonton.

Allan's father, a barber turned implement dealer, was wiped out in the Depression. A lot of people owed him money and, when the Alberta government imposed a moratorium on the collection of farmers' debts, he had to abandon his business and take a job as a salesman to help support his large family. Young Allan often accompanied his father when he made calls on customers, and he says he learned a great deal from the experience.

"Despite ill health and a bad financial situation, my father had a wonderful sense of humour," he says. "Dad was always pleasant, always had a joke for his customers. They liked him – they couldn't help liking him – and they bought things that I'm sure they wouldn't have bought if he hadn't been so darn nice. The biggest thing I learned on those business trips with Dad was that it really behooves us to be pleasant with people. If you're known as having a sense of humour, people *want* to spend time with you. It's as plain as can be – humour breaks down a lot of barriers."

In Edmonton, Al Wachowich belonged to two minority groups – people of Polish origin and Roman Catholics. He went to Catholic schools – most of his friends attended public schools – and he was active in sports, especially baseball and basketball. He later became a Class A basketball referee, a pursuit that brought him into contact with many people throughout Alberta and no doubt heightened his ability to make quick decisions. Al's older brother and former law partner, Ed Wachowich, who's a Provincial Court Judge in Edmonton, recalls the time an angry Calgary sports columnist denounced the officiating of "the world's worst referee, Ed Wachowich." This prompted Ed to say to his kid brother: "Thanks a lot. You borrow my car to go to the game in Calgary, and you borrow my name while you're at it."

For five years, when he was a youngster, Al Wachowich served Mass regularly for Most Reverend Hugh John MacDonald, Archbishop of Edmonton. Like a lot of altar boys, he gave serious consideration to joining the priesthood. Indeed, a quarter-century later, when he was sworn in as a judge, he revealed that his earliest ambition was not to be a lawyer and then a judge, but a priest and then a cardinal. He didn't say whether he aimed even higher. Though he later chose law, he has continued to serve the church in many ways, at the parish level and beyond. In 1972 he was appointed President in Canada of the Canadian Catholic Organization for Development and Peace. One of the "perks" was a private audience with Pope Paul VI.

One of Al Wachowich's best friends was the late Mr. Justice Donald Bowen of the Court of Queen's Bench of Alberta. Bowen, a tough judge and a Presbyterian to boot, used to tease Al about "meddling in church affairs." Wachowich would retaliate, calling Bowen a cold, heartless Protestant who was flirting with hellfire. On and on the evenly matched battle went, until one day, in Rome, "the Polish Prince" fired a royal shot that put him ahead on points.

Shortly after his chat with the Pope, Al Wachowich sent a postcard to his pal Bowen. It read: "Dear Don – His Holiness asked about you. I had to tell him. He said he wasn't surprised."

Al Wachowich was admitted to the bar of Alberta in 1959 and began practising in Edmonton with his brother Ed and Constantine Kosowan, who is now the Chief Judge of the Provincial Courts of Alberta. In 1975, at the tender age of thirty-nine, he was appointed to the District Court of the District of Northern Alberta – the first lawyer of Polish origin to be appointed to the District Court bench in that province.

At the swearing-in ceremony, which was conducted before a full house, speaker after speaker paid tribute to the new judge's industry, pleasant personality, and well-known sense of humour. Rituals of this sort are usually solemn and stuffy, but not this one! It was jocular, nostalgic, anecdotal, affectionate. The jokes flew thick and fast. Each speaker, it seemed, was trying to out-Wachowich Wachowich.

In the course of his light-hearted but sometimes-serious address, the guest of honour stated: "I have learned to treat court matters seriously but, more important, I have learned to have fun and to laugh at myself on occasion as I recall the words of a friend who reminded me, or cautioned me, 'Don't lose this attribute, Wachowich.' " In keeping with this sound advice, he poked fun at his dismal performance in the Appellate Division of the Supreme Court of Alberta – "one win, seventeen losses, and one tie" – and Chief Justice William A. McGillivray quipped, "Don't think that your track record before the Appellate Division is necessarily a thing of the past."

Four years later, Judge Wachowich's judicial track record was sound enough but his membership in the District Court was a thing of the past. That was because the District Court no longer existed. The Supreme Court of Alberta was reconstituted and renamed – the Trial Division was to be called the Court of Queen's Bench, and the Appellate Division would be known as the Court of Appeal. The lower-level District Court was, in effect, "swallowed up" by the higher court, along with all its members. Al Wachowich was no longer "Your Honour" and "Judge" Wachowich. He was now "Your Lordship" and "Mr. Justice" Wachowich.

With the exception of news stories about court cases, there's usually little reason for the media to mention the names of Canadian judges. In Edmonton, though, it's somewhat different in the case of Mr. Justice Allan Wachowich. Reporters always have their ears cocked for Wachowich witticisms when he speaks at charity dinners and other functions, and from time to time there are communiqués concerning the shenanigans of His Lordship and his buddy Al McCann.

On the radio, Edmonton disc jockey Wes Montgomery frequently tells stories about his friend Wachowich. On one occasion Montgomery, stumped by the pronunciation of the name of a performer whose record he was about to play, announced in desperation that it was the work of "Al Wachowich, the Polish Prince." Impressed by the number, several listeners jotted down the name and rushed out to buy it. But, son of a gun, they couldn't find it anywhere in town.

Mr. Justice Wachowich has a couple of rules pertaining to humour. "I never try to make anything funny out of a sensitive situation," he says, "and I'll only joke with people I like. If I kid you, that's a sign that I like you."

If that's the case, he must be positively mad about Ray Jauch, former coach of the Edmonton Eskimos football team. For years, Wachowich and Jauch have waged an "ethnic war" that has brought them both great pleasure.

"I want to make one thing clear," His Lordship said for the record. "Jauch started the ethnic war. Knowing that I'm part Ukrainian, he sent me a record by a fellow named Nestor Pistor – 'The Twelve Days of Christmas,' sung with a thick Ukrainian accent and making slurs about those good people. Naturally, I had to strike back."

Naturally.

Ray Jauch was born in Iowa, but his parents came from Germany. Because of the latter fact, and, of course, because Al Wachowich was fond of him, Jauch was favoured repeatedly with such terms of endearment as "Kraut" and "Square Head." He, in turn, demonstrated his abiding affection for Al by referring to him incessantly as a "dumb Polack." Oh, it was wonderful to see and hear the love these fellows had for each other!

After he'd received the Nestor Pistor record, Mr. Justice Wachowich fashioned a special gift for Jauch – a square-headed football helmet, decorated with swastikas. Thoughfully, he held off sending his token of esteem until April 20 – Adolf Hitler's birthday.

One good turn deserves another, so Jauch sent His Lordship a "Polish golf ball," painted green for ready recognition. On another April 20, Jauch received a swastika-festooned square football, and shortly thereafter Wachowich was given a primitive contraption made from a clothespin and identified as a "Polish switchblade."

And so it went – a square-barrelled shotgun, a "Polish pencil," a square-headed golf club, a "Polish calculator." There was no end to the imagination and inventiveness of these dear friends.

Wachowich and Jauch love duck-hunting, so it was natural that, one April 20, Al sent Ray a beautiful wooden duck decoy. It was square, of course, and embellished with swastikas. When Jauch went to Winnipeg to coach the Blue Bombers, he took all his Wachowich memorabilia with him. The duck was partially destroyed in a fire, and when the fire chief saw the insignias on the charred remains he was gravely concerned about the affiliations of the new football general.

"Where did you get this?" he asked suspiciously.

"From a friend," Jauch replied.

"Who?"

"Mr. Justice Wachowich, in Edmonton."

"A judge wouldn't do a thing like that. I'm going to call him for verification."

The fire chief phoned Mr. Justice Wachowich and told him the situation.

"Do you think a judge would do a thing like that?" Wachowich asked. "I don't even know Mr. Jauch."

Jauch called the mischief-maker a few minutes later and asked him to come clean. Good friend that he was, he did.

It would be a big mistake to leap to the conclusion that Mr. Justice Allan Wachowich is all fun and games. "He's a good judge and he has an informed and incisive legal mind," says one of his fellow jurists. "He's so witty, but he can also be so tough," says Edmonton court reporter Doreen Johnson. "He can really lambaste when he wants to. He's totally down-to-earth. He doesn't have his nose stuck up in the air."

Outside of court – and occasionally in court, if the circumstances are right – His Lordship likes to engage in some good-natured kidding. He often pokes fun at himself, as he does when he tells the long-standing story of how he got his name. "My name's really Walker," he says, "but I changed it to Wachowich so I could get lots of work from the Polacks and the Ukrainians." When he was sworn in as a judge, he told the overflow crowd of well-wishers, "There's absolutely no truth to the rumour that now that I have my appointment I'll be changing my name back to Walker."

One of the parties to a lawsuit, a woman who was representing herself, appeared one morning before Mr. Justice Wachowich and asked for permission to change her name on the documents. "I've remarried," she said, "and my name is no longer Walker."

"You might be in for better times," commented the judge. "My name used to be Walker and I changed it – and look at how well *I'm* doing." The woman didn't have the slightest idea what he was talking about.

Many of the "Wachowich stories" have an ethnic theme. A few years ago, two young thugs beat up two teenagers at a party and stole their money. The next day, when arresting one of the accused, police found he was carrying the same denominations of bills as those that were stolen. Defence counsel called the accused's girlfriend to the stand. She testified that earlier in the evening she had given the accused the contents of his paycheque, which were bills of similar denominations.

"She was an attractive blonde with a Polish name, Pisurski," Mr. Justice Wachowich says, "and I learned that the accused had been living with her. I found him guilty and sentenced him to eight months. The Crown asked for only six months. After the trial, defence counsel asked me why the sentence was two months higher than had been sought. I told him, 'six months for the robbery and two months for sleeping with the Polish girl.'"

Corinne Skura, His Lordship's secretary, says "it's a joy" to work for him. "He always makes my day brighter with his sense of humour," she says. "If I have a problem, he's got an ear. It seems he's always got something to smile about, which is remarkable when you consider the load he carries. In a profession that's concerned with such serious matters, he never fails to see the funny side of things. There's no doubt about it – the self-named Polish Prince touches the lives of all who know him."

Mr. Justice Wachowich talks a great deal about "breaking down barriers" – specifically, barriers based on culture, age, and gender. He knows what it's like to be a member of a minority group, and through his wit and, yes, his tomfoolery, he undoubtedly helps people to loosen up and, in the process, shed some of their alleged superiority. Make no mistake about it, he works at it. It's a mission – a very worthwhile mission.

The Golden Rule gets a good workout when Mr. Justice Wachowich is around. "Young lawyers, especially young women lawyers, are sometimes given a hard time by judges," he notes. "I try to do the opposite, so they won't be too fearful. Lawyers have such heavy responsibilites as it is. Add fear to the picture and you've got an almost intolerable situation. It makes a lot of sense for judges to give some assistance to younger lawyers. The public would be better served and we'd end up with a marvellous bar."

Al Wachowich has done wonders for the camaraderie of Edmonton's bench and bar. The annual "game dinner," which he and his brother Ed started in 1965, has become one of the jolliest shindigs in the city.

"It started out as a very small event," His Lordship says. "In the spring, some of our hunting colleagues decided to get all of their game together and have it cooked, because refrigeration in those days was such that it wasn't wise to keep game too long. The first dinner was in our dining room and my mother was the cook. From then on it was held in a restaurant. It's grown and grown and become a really big event. Ninety-eight percent of the people who attend are from the legal profession, and we have a few invited guests. There's a toast to the game and a reply to that toast, and then we all have a grand time.

"No one has to worry about who's who. Judges, lawyers, law students – everyone's on a first-name basis. The whole evening is light-hearted and good-humoured. There's good food and drink and plenty of fun. It's the kind of evening that lawyers and judges used to have a long time ago."

Before Judge Al Wachowich moved in, the Edmonton courthouse was a pretty staid place. "The judges had never had a party before," he says, "except for a few quiet get-togethers at Christmastime."

The new judge took office on January 10, 1975. Less than two months later, on March 4, the District Court and Supreme Court judges got together in the courthouse to celebrate the feast of St. Casimir, the patron saint of Poland. On May 7 they met again, this time to hoist a few in memory of St. Stanislaus – Poland's most popular saint. Before then, on March 17, St. Patrick was honoured. On that occasion, the Polish Prince, decked out in green leotards, green hat, and green shoes, played a merry leprechaun. At the judges' Christmas party in 1975 – and every year thereafter – Wachowich starred as the "Polish Santa Claus." His uniform consisted of long red underwear, hockey pants, and rubber boots.

Now everyone's in on the act. Once a year, each judge is the guest of honour at a party commemorating his or her ethnic origin. Guests receive modest but appropriate gifts and are then "roasted" by their colleagues. At a recent conclave, Mr. Justice William Haddad, a gentleman of Lebanese lineage, was presented with a fez and a small flying carpet. One St. Patrick's Day, Mr. Justice Michael O'Byrne was awarded a sack of potatoes and a barrage of anti-Irish one-liners. On June 24, 1986 – St-Jean-Baptiste Day – the judges honoured Mr. Justice René Foisy, the one-man Royal Commission on a tragic western rail-crash. Along with a lot of lip, he received an engineer's hat and a record of a dandy ditty entitled "Freight Train, Freight Train, Goin' So Fast."

English, Irish, Welsh, Scots, Lebanese, Jews, Ukrainians, Poles, French Canadians – they've all had their innings, they've all suffered the slings and arrows of outrageous heckling. And they keep coming back for more. As Mr. Justice Wachowich puts it, "We get together and we laugh together." He's proud of the "team" and the progress that's been made on the multicultural front. "You know," he says, "we've broken down a lot of barriers around here."

Judge Ed Wachowich is such a good hunter and accurate shot that his kid brother, Mr. Justice Al Wachowich, calls him "the fastest gun in the West." With a firearm, perhaps, but when it comes to shooting from the lip, few, if any, can beat Al to the draw.

In a recent matrimonial case, an evangelist who'd been married for sixty-six years contended that he shouldn't have to share any of his money with his estranged wife. His cash weighed in at $120,000, the result, he said, of contributions made by appreciative parishioners. "After all," he testified, "it was God's money and my money – and I decided that fifty percent was for God and fifty percent was for me."

At the end of three days of testimony, Mr. Justice Wachowich performed what might be called a judicial miracle. Turning to the husband, he said, "Remember that money you held in your account which you said was half yours and half God's?"

"Yes, of course I do."

"Well, watch carefully, because God's money is about to become your wife's money."

"I had to apologize to God for this," His Lordship said later.

A few years ago Mr. Justice Wachowich tried a case in which, he says, "the scales of justice were completely balanced." *Someone* had to win, but he couldn't make up his mind one way or the other. He thought about it long and hard, then decided in favour of "the fellow who didn't wear an earring."

Before the start of a trial at Vegreville, Alberta, Mr. Justice Wachowich asked both counsel to come to his office to discuss a few matters pertaining to the case. He knew one of the lawyers, Mike Kawulych, but he'd never met the other man, R. D. Hurdle from nearby Vermilion. Kawulych introduced Hurdle, and the judge quickly forgot the name.

At the opening of court, there was the following zippy exchange:

"Are you ready to proceed, Mr. Kawulych?"

"Yes, My Lord."

"Are you ready, Mr. Humble?"

"It's Hurdle, My Lord."

"I wasn't talking to you, Mr. Hurdle. I was talking to myself. Now, are *you* ready, Mr. Hurdle?"

"Yes, sir."

"Good. Then let's proceed."

Yes, sir, it's hard to get the last word with the Polish Prince. He's living proof of the truth of that old saying, "Never kid a kidder." If you want further evidence, Mr. Justice Joseph Bernard Feehan has this to offer:

"Divorces in Edmonton usually started at one-thirty in the afternoon. Wachowich, who was assigned to Divorce Court, was seen walking down the hallway at two o'clock. Someone asked him, 'How come you're finished already?'

"Wachowich said, 'It's because of the way I do them. I have all the Catholics stand on one side of the courtroom and all the Protestants stand on the other side. I grant instant divorces to all the Protestants and I send all the Catholics back for mediation.'

"The fellow asked, 'If that's so, then how come it took you till two o'clock?' Wachowich said, 'There was one Jew.' "

11

"May It Please Your Lordship..."

How sweet and gracious, even in common speech,
Is that fine sense which men call Courtesy!
                    –JAMES THOMAS FIELDS *(1817–1881)*

Manners maketh man.
                    –WILLIAM OF WYKEHAM *(1324–1404)*

The late Nick Skowronski would have agreed with these chaps.

Skowronski, a huge, jolly fellow who owned about sixty percent of the taxicabs in Ottawa, saw more of court in a couple of decades than many lawyers see in a career. In the 1960s and '70s, Nick was hauled into court with great regularity for alleged violations of the criminal law and municipal by-laws – mostly the latter – and one of the biggest lessons he derived from all this travail was that when you're in a jam it doesn't hurt a bit to be oh-so polite. When Skowronski was polite – which, in court, was always – he was a scream.

To better appreciate some of Nick's performances at the bar of justice, let's eavesdrop briefly on a speech made by Cornwall, Ontario, lawyer Thomas R. Swabey. Tom used to be a Provincial Court Judge in Ottawa and, as such, had more than a nodding acquaintance with the engaging Mr. Skowronski.

"The legal profession has a language and manner all its own," Swabey told his listeners. "A great deal of pomp and ceremony accompanies our courts of law. I sometimes feel that the general public, in overhearing the courtroom exchanges of the legal profession, must get the impression that we lawyers are all a bunch of Victorian dandies, for the language and manners of the courtroom, while providing a civil means of communication between adversaries, could be misinterpreted as coming from persons who powder their noses together in the washroom.

"We bow and curtsy to each other and to the judge throughout a trial while prancing around in long black gowns and other finery. We refer to each other as 'my learned friend.' We preface our remarks to the judge with 'may it please Your Lordship' or 'may it please Your Honour,' and we prostrate ourselves with terms like 'with the greatest respect' and 'I beg the court's indulgence.'

"Now, while there is a good reason for all this flowery language – to preserve the dignity of the law and decorum of the courts – it wouldn't be surprising to find that laymen are taken aback by all this mamby-pamby in the courtroom, which is, after all, an arena where the parties are supposedly at each other's throats over some dispute they have brought to the court to be resolved."

Nick Skowronski was a proud man – proud, especially, of his success in the world of commerce. And rightly so. After all, he could neither read nor write. He was proud of his lack of education, too.

"How far did you go in school, Mr. Skowronski?" a judge once asked.

"Our Lordship," Nick replied. "I finished grade two, but it took me four years to do it!"

For the first few years of his marathon war with the authorities, whenever Nick Skowronski went to court he brought a top-flight lawyer with him. He always watched and listened carefully, and when he figured he had the hang of things he started acting for himself.

Skowronski never did get the hang of court lingo. "When Nick addressed the court, it sounded like he was praying," the former Judge Swabey notes. "He usually began by saying, 'May it make Our Honour happy,' then he'd swing into a colourful explanation of his version of the issues before the court, punctuated from time to time with additional adorations, such as 'Our Lordship,' 'Our Excellency,' and 'Our Learned Worship.'

"It was hard to become upset with Nick or annoyed at the frequency of his appearances in court," Swabey says. "He had a manner about him that amused and sometimes attracted sympathy. He was always friendly, never offensive. This disposition was perhaps enhanced by his enormous size – he weighed three hundred pounds – and his ruddy complexion. You always had the feeling that Santa Claus was on trial."

Swabey figures Nick must have been a Catholic, for when he bowed and scraped, which he did at the opening of court and before and after every recess, his right knee would dip a bit, as if he were starting to genuflect but thought there was no need to go *that* far. "I always had the feeling that Nick would have felt more comfortable if there'd been a ring for him to kiss at this point," Swabey says. "No presiding judge could bring himself to do anything but suitably acknowledge this with a solemn, if not clerical, bow."

Swabey recalls a case in which he was presiding and Skowronski was defending himself.

"We were in brand new facilities that weren't quite completed, and when court recessed there was no coffee available. Nick had coffee and doughnuts sent into my office with a note that someone had written at his request. It said, 'Compliments of Nick Skowronski.' I told my secretary there was no way I could accept. 'Don't worry,' she said, 'Mr. Skowronski told me to tell you that he also sent coffee and doughnuts to the Crown Attorney and all the people in the different court offices here.' "

Every Boxing Day, Nick Skowronski had flowers delivered to all the Provincial Court judges in Ottawa.

"The flowers would arrive by taxi," Swabey recalls, "and they always looked as if they were a couple of days old. They were! A court official made some inquiries and learned that Nick got these flowers, cut-rate, from a funeral home. He used to pick the flowers up after they'd been put on the graves, and then he'd rearrange them and have them delivered to the judges."

It's really no wonder that people who aren't too familiar with court find it hard to understand some of the expressions employed by lawyers and judges. Take, for example, the word "brother," which judges often use when referring to each other. Judge Jones might refer to Judge Smith as 'my brother Smith."

In a 1979 case heard in Toronto by Judge Robert B. Dnieper, we get the following dialogue:

Q. It's a public-mischief charge you are on probation for, isn't it, sir?
A. When I went to court that's what I went for, and for driving while disqualified, and Judge Addison –
THE COURT: What did His Honour do?
A. He put me on probation – that's what I'm in court for, the driving charge. He gave me sixty days and two years' probation. I got two years' probation.
THE COURT: My brother Addison put you on probation?
A. No, Judge Addison.

THE COURT: That's my brother Addison.
A. That's your *brother*? I didn't know that.

"My friend" and "my learned friend" are expressions that throw a lot of witnesses and spectators. Former Judge Tom Swabey put it nicely when he said, "You're really taken aback when you hear your hired gun calling your opponent's lawyer his 'learned friend.' 'My God,' you say to yourself, 'this is too much! He's either sold out on me or he's a first-rate liar. Here he is calling this guy his "learned friend" when he told me in his office that the guy's a dimwit that he has no regard for. What's going on here? Have these fellows become bosom buddies all of a sudden?'"

In another Toronto case a defence lawyer, who moments before had concluded a lengthy snarling match with the Crown Attorney, referred to his opponent repeatedly as "my friend." The witness he'd been examining interrupted him finally and asked incredulously, "He's your *friend*?"

C. Maxwell Lane of St. John's spent fourteen years as a magistrate in Newfoundland outports. He says that he and his colleagues were always called "Me Honour." In one case, Lane fined a man twenty dollars. The fellow quipped, "That's no problem, Me Honour. I've often lost more than that on a pair of deuces."

Mr. Justice Nathaniel S. Noel of the Supreme Court of Newfoundland recalls a case he had when he was a practising lawyer. The plaintiff described his injuries and told of an easy, but temporary, job he'd been working at since his accident. Chief Justice Sir Albert Walsh said, "Of course, your regular job would pay better." The man replied, "No, sir, Me Laird, Yer Honour, you gets more money for the easier jobs."

Newfoundland District Court Judge Seamus B. O'Regan writes: "An Irish tavern-owner from St. John's was testifying for the Crown in a case before the Provincial Court. It was obvious that he'd 'taken a few' before coming to court. He prefixed each of his responses to questions from the prosecutor with the phrase, 'Well, Me Lordship, me old cock . . .'
"The prosecutor finally warned him that the proper way of addressing the judge was to say 'Your Honour.' At this stage, the gentleman turned to the judge and said, 'My apologies, Your Honour, me old cock.'"

In Newfoundland, "me old cock" and "me old trout" are practically terms of endearment. A fellow testifying for the defence in another St. John's case, heard in 1975, replied affirmatively to a series of questions asked by Magistrate Hugh O'Neill. "That's right, me old trout," he said several times in a row, then brought the house down with, "That's right, Your Honour, me old trout."

St. John's lawyer James J. Greene, Q.C., told me he once heard a witness call the judge "Your Godship."
   "The judge didn't complain," Jim added. "I think he rather liked it."
   "No wonder," I said, "he'd just had a big promotion."

There are also rules of etiquette governing how to address a judge and his wife in a totally non-court situation and, I ask you, must the average bloke be expected to know *these*, too? For example, if you were sending a Christmas card or an invitation to Judge John Jones and his missus, you'd write "Judge John Jones and Mrs. Jones." If Jones is a member of the highest court of one of our provinces, or, perchance, the Supreme Court of Canada, you'd write "Mr. Justice John Jones and Mrs. Jones."
   Lawyer Ronald F. MacIsaac of Victoria writes: "Herb Wood, who was a long-time magistrate in Vancouver, was elevated to the Supreme Court of British Columbia. On his first judicial trip up into the Cariboo (cowboy country) he and his wife checked into one of the western-style hotels. Signing the book, he wrote, 'Mr. Justice and Mrs. Wood.'
   " 'Oh, no!' said the clerk. 'You'll have to take separate rooms!' "

Now let's look at the other side of the coin.
   This might come as a shock to you, but not everyone who opens his or her mouth in court says nice things. Yes, sir, some folks get very cheeky indeed. And when they do, they run the risk of being tossed in the clink for contempt of court.
   Judge Patrick H. Curran of Halifax tells of a couple of lawyers who got a mite lippy with one of his fellow judges. Fortunately for the lawyers, in each case the judge refrained from retaliating.
   "A man was charged with refusing to take the breathalyzer test," Judge Curran writes, "and the Crown seemed to have an open-and-shut case. However, counsel for the defence argued strenuously that his client was a man of deep religious conviction and had refused to comply with the demand for breath samples because of a Biblical admonition that no man give up his bodily fluids to another.

"The judge said, 'That may well be, counsel, but I'm required to base my decisions on the Criminal Code, not the Bible.'

" 'I understand perfectly, Your Honour,' counsel replied. 'I told my client before we came in here today that the Word of God wouldn't mean anything in your court.' "

The other skirmish arose in the shoplifting trial of a man who was well known as a petty thief. "The accused took the stand and offered a version of the events that would have rendered him innocent," Judge Curran says.

Persons convicted of crime and about to be sentenced sometimes address the court in rather uncomplimentary terms, and it's not always easy for the judge to decide what to do about it. A classic example of this is a case heard a few years back by Judge Robert Dnieper of Toronto.

"Is there anything you wish to say before I sentence you?" Judge Dnieper asked the accused.

"Yeah – fuck you!"

His Honour swung his chair around and, back turned to his tormentor, stared at the wall. And stared. And stared. And thought. And thought. ("What do you say to a bastard like this?" he must have asked himself. "What, if anything, will he *understand?*")

Four or five minutes later, Judge Dnieper swivelled back into position, glared at the accused, and said: "Fuck you, too!"

Court reporter Jack Gordon of Hanover, Ontario, practised his profession for several years in the criminal courts of Toronto. He recalls a woman who totally forgot her manners when appearing before the aforementioned Judge Dnieper. The accused was an elderly prostitute who'd been interrupted at work by a zealous policeman who whisked her off to court, attired only in her housecoat.

"Is there anything you wish to say before sentence is imposed?" Judge Dnieper asked.

The woman whipped open her grubby garment and told His Honour: "Kiss this, Bob!"

Justice of the Peace Peter Breen of Toronto tells a story of a judge who asked the accused what he wanted to say before the passing of sentence. The accused launched into a long story of woe, and the judge told him to confine himself to the highlights. The man disregarded the request and related every bad break he'd had in the last ten years.

"No, no, no," said the judge, holding up his hand like a traffic cop. "I have a quotation for you. I want you to listen to this carefully. 'Laugh, and the world laughs with you; weep, and you weep alone.' – Ella Wheeler Wilcox."

"And I have a quotation for you," said the accused.

"What is it?" asked the judge.

" 'Fuck you!' – Tennessee Williams."

Anytime, anywhere, naughty words might fill the air.

Mr. Justice Douglas H. Carruthers of the Supreme Court of Ontario tells of a murder case heard recently in Windsor. The accused, sick of hearing one witness after another say he was a very bad apple, leaped to his feet and screamed, "You're all a bunch of no-good, rotten bastards!" Then, realizing the likely consequence of his outburst, he turned immediately to the trial judge, Mr. Justice Coulter Osborne, and said, "But not you, Your Lordship!"

12

Watch Your Language!

POLONIUS: What do you read, my Lord?
HAMLET: Words, words, words.

– WILLIAM SHAKESPEARE, *Hamlet*

Poor, pitiful Hamlet! The *problems* that man had!

He'd had it up to here with the slings and arrows of outrageous fortune, he'd spent tons of time trying to decide whether to be or not to be, and then, as if he didn't have enough troubles already, he suddenly realized that he'd lost his appetite for words. They weren't beautiful creatures any more, each with its own special individuality. No, they were just "words, words, words." No wonder he did himself in!

You can hardly get away from words, you know. They're all around you, almost everywhere you look. And, make no mistake about it, they can cause a lot of trouble. Especially if you don't know what the hell they mean.

Take Yogi Berra, for example. If he'd played baseball the way he spoke, his lifetime batting average would have been about .091. Yogi says many wacky things, not because he's stupid – stupid he ain't – but because he doesn't grasp the *meaning* of certain words and uses 'em anyway. A couple of samples will suffice: "You can observe a lot just by watching"; and, on another occasion, "Mantle can hit just as good right-handed as he can left-handed. He's just naturally amphibious."

You get the idea. If you don't know what makes them tick, words can blow up in your face. And that's doubly true for testifying in court. If you're going to be giving any testimony, be sure you understand what the questioner is driving at. If a word has you stumped, say so. Get the matter cleared up before you move on. If you don't, you might end up in my next book.

Way back in ancient times, a fellow named Hippocrates observed: "The chief virtue that language can have is clearness, and nothing detracts from it so much as the use of unfamiliar words."

Hippocrates must have spent a fair bit of time in court. The condition he describes is the source of much legal humour.

"Did the accused ejaculate?" a Toronto prosecutor asked the complainant in a sexual assault case.
　　"Pardon?"
　　"Did he ejaculate?"
　　"Jack *who*?"

Ron Paskar, a Mississauga, Ontario, law student, was in Sudbury recently and heard the following courtroom dialogue:

This next person, a university student in Ontario, must have been so tuckered out that she didn't know what she was saying.

Q. How many courses did you take in the summer? Two?
A. Two courses. Two half-courses in philosophy and one intercourse in psychology.
Q. Did you, in fact, get credit for those two courses?
A. I did, yeah.
Q. So does that represent one to two complete courses toward the first year of a degree?
A. It does, yes.
Q. What are you taking over the fall and winter term?
A. I'm taking an intercourse in philosophy, an intercourse in social work, and an intercourse in sociology.

In Orangeville, Ontario, a woman hauled her husband into court to determine why he was behind in his support payments.

"I can't pay because I'm going to university," the man told the judge. "I just have to raise my intuition fees."

Pat Sullivan, a former legal secretary from Truro, Nova Scotia, recalls a case in which a farmer said, "Ever since my father became decapitated, he's useless on the farm."

Judge Felix A. Cacchione of Halifax remembers an armed robbery case in which the accused told the police he was prepared to take "a lie protector test."

"I enjoy listening for the funny things people say in court when they are nervous or trying to use their very best language," writes Judge Norris Weisman, of the Provincial Court (Family Division) in Toronto. Judge Weisman has collected a great many gems. Here are a few:

- "My wife has a speech impeachment."
- "I get a free apartment with all the infringements."
- "I was standing in the foynier. I saw her coming in aliberated. But I don't want the kid mangled up in this."
- "This man was going around with my alias."
- "My kid had impetango."

MY KID HAD IMPETANGO.

I'M TAKING AN INTERCOURSE IN PHILOSOPHY. AN INTERCOURSE IN SOCIAL WORK AND AN INTERCOURSE IN SOCIOLOGY.

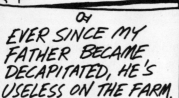

EVER SINCE MY FATHER BECAME DECAPITATED, HE'S USELESS ON THE FARM.

THIS MAN WAS GOING AROUND WITH **MY** ALIAS.

I KNOW YOU BELIEVE YOU UNDERSTAND WHAT YOU THINK I SAID BUT I'M NOT SURE YOU REALIZE THAT WHAT YOU HEARD IS NOT WHAT I MEANT.

- "I seek apathy from the court."
- "The Children's Aid Company took the children."
- Social worker: "Access should be in the discrimination of the Children's Aid Society."
- "My boy needs help. He should be seen by a good gynecologist."

Judge Weisman's colleague, Judge Stewart Fisher of Etobicoke, Ontario, sums up utterances such as these in the following lingo: "I know you believe you understand what you think I said, but I'm not sure you realize that what you heard is not what I meant."

If everyone always said exactly what they meant, we'd have a lot fewer laughs. Long may "the right word" be wide of the target!

Eric D. McCooeye, a lawyer in Sault Ste. Marie, Ontario, tells of a divorce case based on cruelty. The judge asked the petitioner to give some details of her husband's misconduct, and she replied: "The worst thing he did was kick me in the gentiles."

London, Ontario, lawyer Ted Madison acted for a child who'd been bitten on the top front of his thigh by a dog. The boy's parents sued the dog's owner, and the case was eventually settled and approved by a judge. The boy's father, pleased with the outcome, told Madison: "Freddy was lucky. Four inches more and the dog would have bitten his genials."

Frank Maczko, Q.C., secretary of the Law Society of British Columbia, used to be director of the B.C. Legal Aid Society. After he took off for a year of studies at the London School of Economics, the switchboard at Legal Aid received a call for him.

"He's on leave for a year," the operator said.

"Where's he gone?" the caller asked.

"To England."

"Why?"

"He's taking a sabbatical."

"A sabbatical? I didn't even know he was Jewish!"

When you're testifying, you have to listen ever so carefully to the questions – like this woman in Fort McMurray, Alberta:

"You're the mother of the children?"

"Yes, sir."

"Is there a lawful marriage?"

"Yes, I was m . . . Did you saw lawful or awful?"

Mr. Justice Melvin E. Shannon of the Alberta Court of Queen's Bench sends this linguistic tidbit:

LAWYER: What did your husband do to you?
WITNESS: He called me a lot of profound names.
JUDGE: Madam, are you sure that you mean profound? Could it be that you mean profane?
WITNESS: Profound or profane, whatever.
JUDGE: Well, how about profoundly profane?
WITNESS: That's it, that'll do.

Joel E. Pink, Q.C., of Halifax tells the sad tale of a motorist whose mouth was even faster than his car. The man was clocked at seventy-two kilometres per hour in a fifty-kilometre zone. It was a bright, sunny day, with no sign of other cars or pedestrians.

The accused's lawyer explained that, under Nova Scotia law, a speeder who drove under eighty kilometres per hour could still beat the rap if he established to the satisfaction of the court that he drove "carefully and prudently" in the circumstances.

The lawyer drilled that phrase – "carefully and prudently" – into his client's head. "Don't forget," he reminded him for the umpteenth time, "when I ask you how you were driving you should say 'carefully and prudently,' if that's true."

"I've got it, I've got it," the client assured him.

In the courtroom, the lawyer guided his client through his testimony, then asked the Big Question: "How would you say you were driving?"

"Carelessly and imprudently," came the instant reply.

"Guilty!" came the instant verdict.

Look, I wouldn't want to create the impression that witnesses are the only ones who get balled up with words. Lawyers are pretty good at that too.

Judge Felix A. Cacchione recalls a rookie prosecutor in Halifax who, in preparing for a rape trial, asked a colleague what he had to prove. "Penetration of the woman's vagina," the older man said. At the preliminary hearing the prosecutor asked the woman, "What, if anything, happened in the area of your regina?"

The Honourable Gordon Cooper, a former judge of the Supreme Court of Ontario, remembers the time a well-known lawyer asked a witness: "Now where were you when the RCMP condescended upon you?"

One of my favourite stories along these lines is of the lawyer who said, "Your Honour, I've made efforts to contact the alleged father, who lives in the alleged state of Wisconsin." In another case, a lawyer whose brain and tongue were out of gear asked the man in the box, "Each year, how many moneys do you averagely receive?"

Sydney, Nova Scotia, lawyer David Muise likes to tell of the time his colleague Joe Rizzetto had some fun in court playing amateur grammarian. One of the parties in a motor-vehicle accident case was describing his driving and the events leading up to the crash.

"What happened next?" asked Rizzetto.

"Well, then I swung around the corner," the witness replied.

"You'll have to excuse this fellow, Your Honour," the lawyer quipped. "He's just an ignorant, uneducated miner. He means he *swang* around the corner."

It's bad enough when they stump you with your own langauge, but when lawyers and judges start tossing in Latin too, what chance has the average bloke got? It's all Greek to him.

Courts don't mess around with Latin anywhere near as much as they used to. But there are certain Latin expressions that pop up often. *Ex parte* is one of them. It means "from one side only" and is applied to a legal proceeding in which only one side of the case is presented and the opposing side is absent. *Viva voce* is another pet phrase. It means "with the living voice" – in a word, orally.

Put 'em together and what do you get? Ask Vancouver lawyer Frank Maczko, Q.C.

"I once interviewed a plumber against whom his wife had obtained an *ex parte* injunction to keep him away from the family home," Frank recalls. "I had forgotten how important it is to translate for clients, and I said to him that I would have to make a motion in chambers to have evidence heard *viva voce*. He gave me a blank stare and said, 'It sounds like you're going for a crap!'"

Sine die is a Latin expression that's used very often in court. It means, literally, "without day," that is, indefinitely. Many a poor soul has run afoul of this innocent-looking expression.

Jacques Gauthier, a lawyer in St. Joseph, New Brunswick, writes: "We have a new sheriff in the Court of Queen's Bench. He is French and helps the judges with introducing cases and administering oaths to witnesses. One day, in the middle of February 1985, during a snowstorm, he announced to the people in court: 'This court is adjourned to a sunny day.' "

Flagrante delicto crops up every now and then. It means "in the commission of the offence." In sex cases it translates, roughly, into "caught with your pants down."

Toronto lawyer John D. Gibson recalls a divorce case he had before Judge (now Mr. Justice) Allan Hollingworth:

"When I asked the usual stock questions of the petitioner as to whether she had any personal knowledge of the adultery of her husband, she answered, much to my amazement, 'I sure do. We were having a party and when I walked into the bedroom to get somebody's coat, there he was going at it.'

"There was tittering in the body of the court, and His Honour's face transformed itself into a beatific smile. He looked down over his glasses at the petitioner and said, 'What, in *flagrante delicto*?' Her reply, given in wide-eyed innocence, brought the house down: 'I guess so.' "

But enough of this Latin falderal. Let's get back to good old simple English.

Chief Judge Harold Gyles, of the Provincial Court (Criminal Division) in Winnipeg, recalls a prosecution brought several years ago against a Winnipeg massage parlour. The authorities alleged it was a common bawdy house.

One of the girls who worked in this establishment was being questioned by the prosecutor as to various services performed on the premises and the fees charged therefor:

13

To Err Is Human

To err is human, and it feels divine.

—MAE WEST

Right on, my little chickadee! Especially when it's someone else's goof.

Let's cavort for a while in the wacky world of boners, boo-boos, and bloopers. Examples thereof abound in our law offices and courthouses, so I suggest we visit a few such establishments and examine some of the incriminating evidence.

I'm indebted to an Ontario judge who sent me a wonderful collection of "dictation gems" compiled by his secretary when he was in practice. He's a great sport and, though he didn't request it, I'm going to cloak him in anonymity. Here are a few of the lulus that sprang from the fertile – and overworked – brain of this nameless learned gentleman:

- "I am writing at this time even though I know you will be away when you receive this letter."
- (The start of an affidavit): "I make oath and say as follows: 1. I am the father of my son."
- "Call Mr. Jones and find out his height, weight, and sex."
- (Memo *re* house deal): "Phone Mrs. Brown and find out if she has gas."
- "We shall expect this to be done within the next week or seven days."
- ". . . And on the weekends starting Monday noon to Friday noon."
- "This woman spokes breaken English."
- (From a memo *re* a statement of claim): "Defendant's vehicle was going in a northerly direction and the plaintiff's vehicle was travelling in a northerly direction, resulting in a head-on collision."
- "He failed to avoid a collision which he saw or ought to have seen was intimate."
- "The defendant died recently. We are having him confirm this."
- "We are enclosing these documents in eskimo."

Oh, well, Your Honour, no one's perfect. As manager Danny Ozark said when his Philadelphia Phillies blew a fifteen-and-a-half-game lead: "Even Napoleon had his Watergate."

When a judge has heard a case and given his decision, he can't erase his verdict and retry the case. To use lingo that's been around for centuries, the judge is *functus officio*. That's Latin for "having discharged his duty." Lawyers and judges often say *functus* for short.

Vancouver lawyer Humphrey E. Waldock had an angry client. The lawsuit was over and she had lost. She urged her lawyer to have the judge reopen the case. He decided to write to her. "I know you are very unhappy with the decision," he dictated, "but, as I said the other day, Judge Jones is *functus*."

The letter awaiting Waldock's signature said, "Judge Jones has fucked us."

Barry A. Spiegel, Q.C., of Toronto tells of a transaction he was involved in a few years ago:

"The lawyer on the other side was from New England and spoke in the traditional clipped manner of that region. When he came to close the transaction, we provided him with the services of one of our secretaries, who became somewhat enamoured of him. She gave herself away when, in response to his dictated 'very truly yours,' she typed 'virtually yours.' "

Spiegel also sends this beaut:

"Some time ago, I had occasion to write a reply to a rather unpleasant lawyer who had written a letter to an associate of mine. I found his letter unfair and his tone impudent and dictated a letter to him, advising accordingly. I had no intention of casting aspersions on his masculinity and was therefore somewhat surprised to find that my young secretary had typed: 'Frankly, I find your impotence unacceptable.' "

Speaking of that sort of thing, we turn now to a notice of motion prepared in a busy law office. As people in legal circles know, a notice of motion is a document in which one party in a court matter notifies an opponent in writing that his or her lawyer will be seeking a particular kind of order from a judge as soon as counsel can be heard on a stated day.

Ronald J. Fromstein, a lawyer in Ajax, Ontario, sent me the notice. It pertained to a motion brought under the Vendors and Purchasers Act, and it read in part as follows:

"TAKE NOTICE that a motion will be made to the court on behalf of the above-named purchasers at the Court House, 605 Rossland Road East, Whitby, on Thursday, the 1st day of September 1983, at 10:00 o'clock in the forenoon, or so soon thereafter as counsel can be hard, for an order declaring . . ."

Continuing in that vein, Anne McIntyre, a lawyer in Fenelon Falls, Ontario, received a draft separation agreement that said the husband was to increase his support payments annually "in accordance with the cost of loving."

London, Ontario, court reporter Gail McGilvray, in preparing the transcript of a doctor's evidence in a civil case, was often called upon to type the words "degenerative disc disease." On the verge of punchiness, and fearing that something might have gone amiss, Gail cast an eagle eye over what she had written. Sure enough, somewhere along the way the plaintiff had contracted a "degenerative dick disease."

En garde! Gail McGilvray also sends this snippet from a letter filed as a court exhibit: "Upon receipt of these funds we will provide you with the discharge of the bank's mortgage, duelly executed."

Who said business is all business? Sometimes there's a musical interlude, according to Toronto lawyer Paul J. Crowe. Paul recently received a draft deed from a law firm acting for a big construction company. The letter said the document would be signed by "an authorized singing officer."

And consider Walkerton, Ontario, lawyer David O. McCray who, a few years back, took instructions from a woman who was making her will. The woman said that she wanted a plaque in her memory at the local hospital. The will, as typed, said she wanted a "plague" in her memory at (of all places!) the local hospital.

It takes a long, long time to reach the top of the legal world. Why, just last year a firm advertised in the Vancouver *Province* for a "junior barrister with forty-three years' experience."

The verbal carnage continues unabated. Dartmouth, Nova Scotia, lawyer Linda M. Tippett recently received a "ruff draft" of a court order for her approval, and Robert F. Evans, who practises in Bradford, Ontario, was sent an affidavit with instructions to have it sworn by his client before "a commissioner of oats."

No one is immune. I have received several letters from people who had nice things to say about my book, "*Court Gestures*."

(Incidentally, even the Bible has had its share of typos. The 1923 edition of the King James Version of the Bible warned that "a man may not marry his grandmother's wife." A couple of letters got transposed in the first Bible printed in Ireland, with the result that, in John 5:14, Christ commanded readers to "sin on more." My favourite, which I try to observe at all times, is the commandment set out in the 1623 printing of the King James Version: "Thou shalt commit adultery.")

Toronto lawyer S. Wayne Morris writes: "A few years ago, a student in our firm was corresponding with a client and intended to say 'Liability, of course, remains an issue.' Instead, the letter went out as follows: "My ability, of course, remains an issue.' "

A summary of a 1984 lawsuit began: "The Bogojevskis were interested in buying a house to be built on a lot and specifically stated that they were only interested in a detached house. They did not speck engligh well and when . . ."

You have no idea of some of the things that happen in courthouses. But Frank Maczko, Q.C., does. It's his job to know; he's secretary of the Law Society of British Columbia.

Frank sent me a newspaper article that described a new Unified Family Court. It read in part: "He [the Attorney General of B.C.] and the other attorneys general visited a pilot family court project in Richmond, a Vancouver suburb, in which a federal and a provincial judge shit in tandem to deal with cases in a comprehensive way."

Crown Counsel Steve Stirling of Port Alberni, British Columbia, writes: "The current round of spying charges reminds me of a case I was involved in, in which a witness testified that he'd seen a dog 'defecting' on his neighbour's lawn." And in another one of Steve's cases, a policeman issued a traffic ticket for "carless driving."

"Onus" is a word that pops up often in criminal law: the Crown has an onus (obligation) to prove guilt beyond a reasonable doubt; the defence has an onus to prove certain things in certain situations.

Well, that's all very well and good, but a fellow can't be blamed for wondering what goes on in Judge Kenneth L. Crockett's courtroom in Edmonton.

One day in 1982, Judge Crockett convicted a man of criminal negligence in the operation of his motor vehicle. The man thought it was a bum decision, so he appealed to a higher court, stating in his notice of appeal that "the learned trial judge placed too heavy an anus on the defence . . ."

Cranbrook, British Columbia, Crown Attorney Richard Cairns sends a transcript of an impaired-driving case heard – appropriately – on April Fool's Day. The evidence reads in part:

CROWN COUNSEL: Circumstances, Your Honour. On February 22, 1986, at approximately 18:45, a vehicle was noted to sway back and forth in its own lane as it went down 68th Avenue. The vehicle was stopped. A moderate odour of liquor was noticed on Mr. Gohn, a flussed flace – flushed face . . .

THE COURT (after hearing the fully litany): Do you have anything you want to say about that?

ACCUSED: Well, I don't quite agree with that, that my splurch was splurred . . .

Newmarket, Ontario, lawyer Daniel W. Monteith tells of a recent impaired-driving appeal in which Crown Counsel, summarizing the evidence, told the court: "The officer could see a strong odour of an alcoholic beverage on the breath of the accused."

Court reporter Jack Gordon of Hanover, Ontario, recalls the time he recorded the evidence in an impaired-driving case brought against a woman. The investigating officer rattled off the usual signs of impairment – glassy eyes, slurred speech, unsteady gait – and then told the court that "there was the smell of liquor on her breast."

Montreal lawyer Manuel Shacter, Q.C., writes: "I recall a client who was discussing estate planning, and in that connection he was thinking about the age at which his children should receive the capital of his estate. After reflecting for a while he exclaimed, "I think it's time to cut the biblical cord."

To slightly rearrange an old saying: There's many a slip twixt the mind and the lip. Janet C. Kelly, a lawyer in Manotick, Ontario, gives an example:

"I had the opportunity to work the summer in Provincial Court (Family Division) in London, Ontario, at which time I had the privilege of making my first court appearance on behalf of a client.

"I expected that my case would be called in the morning and for some considerable time reviewed in my mind that my opening remarks would be 'Good morning, Your Honour, my name is . . . and I represent . . .'

"As the day wore on, this refrain played in my mind over and over, and when I finally entered the courtroom, late in the afternoon, I boldly blurted out: 'Good morning, your afternoon.' "

What better way to close than with an honest-to-God Freudian slip or two?

Judge Norris Weisman, of the Provincial Court (Family Division) in Toronto, recalls a sex-abuse case in which a social worker said on the stand: "A few incidents stick up in my mind."

And court reporter Maria Mihailovich reports that in a recent case in Provincial Court in Hamilton, a young man was charged with the theft of four condoms. Upon reviewing the evidence and noting that the accused had no previous criminal record, the Crown Attorney declared: "Your Honour, I think under the circumstances this is an appropriate case for a discharge." Then she put her hands to her mouth and exclaimed, "Oh, no, did I say that?"

14

Bush-League Justice

It was the rookie's first case, and he was plenty nervous.

"If we're not ready now, we never will be," Douglas G. Haig told his client, that memorable day in 1954. "It's coming up for ten, so we'd better get moving."

Haig closed his shiny new briefcase and he and his client walked briskly up the main street of Midland, Ontario. They were on their way to court.

So, all right, it wasn't the Supreme Court of Canada they were heading for. It wasn't the Supreme Court of Ontario, either, or the County Court of the County of Simcoe. No, it was the lowly Division Court, a Class-D tribunal that's known these days as Small Claims Court. But, listen, when you've just been called to the bar, *any* court, *any* case, can make you break out in hives.

Division Court was held once a month in the Midland council chamber, located over the town firehall. But this particular day, Haig soon learned, the court would have to be held somewhere else.

Judge James Harvie was furious. Upon his arrival, minutes earlier, he'd discovered that the local magistrate was already conducting his own court in the council chamber. Harvie was a judge of the County Court; hearing Division Court cases was a minor part of that position. He outranked the magistrate. Why, he could have told the interloper to buzz off and find another place to hold court.

But Judge Harvie was known far and wide as a gentleman. He didn't want to cause a fuss, so he decided that *he* would dispense justice at another locale.

But where?

"How about the firehall?" the court clerk inquired.

"You mean downstairs?" asked the judge, recoiling at the thought. "With the fire engines and all?"

"Yes, Your Honour. There won't be much room, but we can probably arrange something."

"Well, let's have a look," sighed the judge.

Midland was no one-horse town – its population was 7,500 and climbing – and it wasn't a one-engine town, either. A pair of gleaming fire engines, parked side by side, consumed all but a bit of the space in the town firehall.

The court clerk scared up a card table and a metal chair for the judge and placed them in the narrow "corridor" between the big red machines.

"Where do *we* sit?" asked Oliver H. Smith, Q.C., Haig's worthy opponent.

"There," said the clerk, pointing to a couple of snazzy running boards.

"This is ludicrous, outrageous!" huffed Judge Harvie, who was known hither and yon as a man of great dignity. "Oh, all right, let's give it a try."

The judge took his place at the card table. Off to one side, and slightly ahead of him, Doug Haig lowered his rump onto the running board of one of the fire trucks. Across the way, some five feet "distant," Oliver Smith deposited his bulky frame on the running board of the other machine. They sat facing each other, like a couple of bookends, while the clerk, the parties to the lawsuit, and their witnesses looked for somewhere to loiter.

Smith's client took the "stand" and testified that Haig's client owed him $112.76.

"That's a lie!" Haig's client screamed. His piercing voice caromed off the concrete walls of the firehall and made the judge wince.

"Don't interrupt!" His Honour warned, almost screaming. "You can have your say later!"

But Haig's client kept butting in. "He's a goddamn liar!" he roared in response to one piece of testimony. Twice he almost lunged at the witness, who stood a tantalizing three feet away. He obviously loathed the witness.

It wasn't long before the two were shouting back and forth at each other and pandemonium had taken over the proceedings. Then – merciful heavens! – another voice, far more jarring than the others, joined in the tumult.

The fire-siren atop the building shrieked an ear-splitting message of its own. As the alarm wailed on, Judge Harvie tossed his books and papers in his briefcase and walked calmly through the door. Seconds later, hordes of excited men swarmed into the "courtroom," jumped aboard the fire engines, and zoomed off to do battle with a dreaded foe.

Suddenly, two lawyers, two clients, one court clerk, and an assortment of witnesses found themselves in an empty firehall. They had nowhere to sit, no judge to adjudicate the case, and no idea whether the judge would even be back.

A short time later, the fire engines returned and reclaimed their parking spots. "False alarm," a firefighter said as he hurried back to his regular, paying occupation. After a while, with still no sign of the judge, the clerk adjourned court for a month.

Later that day, Doug Haig's client brought matters to a swift conclusion. He went looking for the other party to the lawsuit, and when he found him he beat the bejabbers out of him. The fellow lost all interest in the case and the trial was never resumed.

And so ends the tale of a rookie's debut in the courts. More than thirty years have slipped by since then, and whenever Douglas G. Haig, Q.C., recalls that fiasco in the firehall – and other wacky wars waged in other offbeat places – he's quick to affirm that in this big, wonderful land one frequently encounters a phenomenon that can best be described as "bush-league justice."

Now don't get me wrong. I'm not saying that we have bush-league *judges*. We've got pretty damn good judges, by and large, but some of the *places* they have to do their judging *in* are fit for neither man nor beast.

Oh, we've got a goodly number of magnificent courthouses and spiffy courtrooms in our main judicial centres – especially those inhabited by judges of our higher courts. But if you were a judge in one of our so-called "lower" courts – where the vast majority of Canadian cases are decided – you wouldn't be too thrilled with some of the dives you're told to toil in. In out-of-the-way places, the facilities are often laughable. Governments don't splurge on justice in the boondocks.

Let's visit some of these neglected outposts of justice, shall we? Let's roam through the hinterland for a spell and take a gander at law in the raw. I've arranged a tour that I hope you'll find both enlightening and entertaining. It starts Down East in, of all places, a firehall.

Toronto criminal lawyer William G. Murphy hails from New Brunswick. He was a prosecutor there for four years before heading for Ontario in 1954. Bill reminisces about the good old days:

"Back in the early 1950s, when I was a Crown Prosecutor in Moncton, I went once every two weeks to a little place called Port Elgin to try cases. There was no television in those days, and people came from far and wide to watch court. They always had a grand time.

"There was no courthouse in the village. Court was held in the firehall. I don't mean over the firehall, or beside the firehall. I mean *in* the firehall.

"They backed the fire engine up as far as they could to allow space for a card table. The justice of the peace would sit at the card table, facing the fire engine. The Crown Prosecutor and defence lawyer would sit on the front bumper of the machine, facing the J.P. You were so close to him you could sit there on the bumper and lean forward onto his table.

"The place was always full of people. They'd be all over the fire truck – accused persons, witnesses, and spectators sitting on every available inch of the truck. There'd be people standing in the narrow spaces beside the truck, and to the sides of the card table."

Murphy says he never had to prosecute anyone for theft or fraud or taking or selling drugs. But assault – well, that was a different kettle of fists. There were plenty of good old-fashioned assault cases for the J.P. to sort out, down at the Port Elgin firehall.

"The folks expected a show, and we always gave them one," Murphy recalls. "What great shows they were! I'd call a witness to testify and he'd scramble down from somewhere on top of the fire engine, just itching to tell about the brawl that Bill and Bob had last Saturday night down by the wharf. He'd say things like 'Bill smashed Bob in the face and then Bob hit him over the head with a lobster trap and then Bill hit Bob in the balls with a big log he found layin' on the ground,' and he'd go on like that until he'd told everything he remembered about the scrap. And the people were crazy about the story that was unfolding – like listening to the fights on the radio. There'd even be cheering and booing, just like at the fights.

"And the lawyers would add to the excitement by pretending to hate each other's guts. We got away with things before that J.P. that we'd never get away with in Moncton, where they had real magistrates. And then the lawyers would have a drink and some laughs when they got to Shediac, on the way back to Moncton. I loved going to that little firehall."

Margaret Graham, who operates a court-reporting service in Dartmouth, Nova Scotia, used to take down the evidence for Provincial Court Judge Leo McIntyre when he held court in various Cape Breton communities. In Cheticamp there was nowhere court could be held except in – you guessed it – the firehall. Judge McIntyre, who retired only a few years ago, presided once a month in that pretty seaside village near Cape Breton Highlands National Park.

"Spectators and witnesses sat on fire trucks to watch the court proceedings," Graham recollects with a smile. "Court was the big excitement in Cheticamp. The people wouldn't miss it for the world, even if they did have to sit on fire trucks to find out what had been going on in their area."

Judge Dwayne Wade Rowe of the Territorial Court of the Yukon also served for a spell on the Provincial Court of Alberta. In his years at the bar he was recognized as one of Alberta's top criminal lawyers. I asked His Honour to rev up his memory and file a report on some of his encounters with bush-league justice.

"As a lawyer and Provincial Court Judge in Alberta, I have been in seventy places where court is held," Judge Rowe states. "In Valleyview, Alberta, the roof leaked and during trials I would, from my vantage point on the bench, direct my clerk in placing wastepaper baskets, buckets, lunchpails, and other containers to catch the drips. In the 1960s, in the Peace River country, we used Legion halls, RCMP barracks, and church basements for court.

"In the Yukon, at Pelly Crossing, two hundred miles north of Whitehorse, the Indian Band Hall is used. In the winter, if the judge isn't too popular at the moment, he arrives at a cold hall in the midst of temperatures around forty-five below. Once, Chief Judge Geoffry Bladon's pen froze. In the summer, children and dogs wander in and out and people outside throw rocks through the open window."

No so long ago, in the village of Barry's Bay in the Ottawa Valley, court was held in a former schoolhouse. The courtroom was heated by an ancient pot-bellied stove, near which was a sign that for many years had been warning folks: "Please Do Not Urinate on the Stove."

One fine spring day, a chicken wandered through the door while court was in session. It strolled around for a while, amusing one and all, and then ambled back outside.

"That chicken must know how to read," a wag in the audience remarked. "Not once did it pee on the stove."

Daphne Zander is clerk of the Provincial Court (Criminal Division) in Pembroke, Ontario, a job that takes her to several Ottawa Valley communities when court is in session. Daphne recalls a case heard a few years ago in the village of Killaloe, population six hundred and change. A man was on trial for fishing out of season. Exhibit A in the proceedings, a fish landed by the accused, lay on a table near Daphne's desk.

At least that's where it was when court recessed at noon. While everyone was at lunch, a ravenous cat happened upon Exhibit A and quickly reduced it to bones.

Cornwall, Ontario, lawyer Thomas R. Swabey was a member of the Provincial Court (Criminal Division) for a decade in the 1960s and '70s. He was stationed in Ottawa, but in the later years of his stint he often heard cases in "the Valley." By the time Tom started going to Killaloe, court was held in the municipal office, a one-room affair with a telephone that couldn't be shut off during deliberations.

Swabey gets the giggles whenever he recalls this palace of justice. "The judge's 'office' was a walk-in vault," he says with a grin. "After a few minutes in there on my 'break' I felt I was going squirrelly. And the bloody phone would ring during court – calls about dog tags and that sort of thing. Right in the middle of someone's evidence, you'd hear the village clerk telling some caller angrily, 'I can't talk to you now. Court's in session.' "

Lawyers sometimes ask the judge to order that witnesses remain outside the courtroom until needed – so they won't be influenced by what others say on the stand. "In Killaloe," Swabey says, "if witnesses were excluded they had to stand outside the building, or sit in cars, until they were called in to testify."

Judge Swabey made the occasional trip to Whitney, a village near the edge of Algonquin Provincial Park. In that community, court was conducted in the parish hall of the Catholic church.

"I always enjoyed going to Whitney," Tom chuckles. "My 'office' there was the tiny kitchen of the parish hall. The parish priest was the 'court clerk,' and he used to bake tea-biscuits and tarts for me in the oven in that little kitchen. He'd have them ready when I arrived, and we'd share a pot of tea and eat some of his goodies before opening court.

"On one of my visits, the court reporter's typewriter was temporarily stashed in the oven – to keep it away from people in court who might be tempted to make off with it. A short time later, the priest came into the kitchen–courtroom, turned on the oven to start baking, and left. Fortunately the reporter realized what had happened, and she rescued her machine. We almost had baked typewriter for lunch."

Rod A. Cormack, Q.C., is a senior counsel in the office of the Attorney General of Ontario. In the late 1950s, when he was a young lawyer practising in Toronto, Rod went to the village of Marmora, near Peterborough, Ontario, to defend a man charged with a criminal offence. "It was a miserable, cold winter's day," he recalls, "with lots of snow on the ground."

Court was held in a one-room schoolhouse. When Cormack arrived, a few minutes before court was to start, a man in a sweater was stoking the pot-bellied stove in the courtroom. The man left briefly, then returned and chatted for a while with the judge. Rod learned later that the man in the sweater was the justice of the peace.

"I ask that witnesses be excluded, Your Honour," Cormack said when the trial got under way.

"Do you really want that?" asked the judge.

"Yes sir."

"You're sure?"

"Yes."

"Very well," the judge replied. He instructed the Crown's first witness to remain in court to testify, then told the three other witnesses to remain outside the courtroom until they were called to give evidence.

After the first witness had told his story, defence counsel grilled him at length. Then the judge told the witness he could leave.

"I call my next witness, John Smith," the prosecutor announced. A short time later Smith reappeared, red-faced and frosty-haired, and took the stand.

In turn, all three witnesses testified and then submitted to lengthy cross-examination by the eager young lawyer from the city. When they re-entered court, all three looked as if they'd been walking around in the cold for a couple of hours.

As a matter of fact, that's what they'd been doing. Cormack didn't know it, but there was nowhere the excluded witnesses could go except outdoors. They'd been stomping their feet and flailing their arms all morning – longing to get back inside that "courthouse" and bask in the glow of its pot-bellied stove.

Of course, there's nothing new about bush-league justice. We've had it since the 1600s. But back in the early days, when everything was new and primitive, you could hardly expect to have ritzy courthouses, could you? Take Newfoundland, for example. The pioneer Newfies had a situation that left a whole lot to be desired.

For a couple of centuries or so, Britain strenuously opposed settlement of the Crown Colony called Newfoundland. Oh, folks could go there and fish all they wanted but, come fall, they had to get the hell out. They could keep coming back every spring, if they wished, as long as they took a powder when fishing was done for the year. As for "law and order," from about 1640 to 1760 the "Fishing Admirals" ran the entire show.

The rigid rule, decreed by the infamous Star Chamber, was that the captain of the first ship to arrive in any particular harbour was to be admiral of that port for the fishing season. This fellow, who might be (and often was) an ignorant bully, had complete power to allot places in the harbour, to act as judge in all cases of dispute, and in general to act as governor, parliament, and law courts combined till it was time for everyone, including him, to hustle back home for the duration.

A Fishing Admiral, no matter how untutored or debased he might be, had almost the power of life and death over hundreds of people who were just trying to make a living. This was the "golden age" of bush-league justice, in every sense of the term. The Fishing Admiral has been described as follows:

"He had to decide matters in which he himself might be involved and in which he would naturally decide in his own favour. The 'courthouse' was usually a fish store where, seated on a barrel, the admiral, who had probably been bribed with money or a bowl of calabogus (a drink composed of rum, spruce beer, and molasses) gave his judgments. Places on the beach were wrongfully wrested from their owners, taken by the admiral, or given to his friends. Those who earned his displeasure were heavily fined or brutally whipped. In addition to all this, he was the importer of all goods necessary for domestic use and also for the fishery, and he sold these at his own prices."

Until about 1939, justice was brought to the Newfoundland outports by sailing ship. Every August a chartered schooner would leave St. John's on a long journey around the island, conveying a judge, court staff, and several lawyers to courts in Burin, Grand Bank, Harbour Breton, Port-aux-Basques, St. George's, Corner Brook, St. Anthony, Twillingate, Trinity, and Clarenville. Chief Justice Alexander Hickman of the Trial Division of the Supreme Court of Newfoundland said that lawyers on the "boat circuit" would often interview clients in the morning, prepare and exchange legal documents by noon, and start trying the lawsuit after lunch. Criminal cases, which required no paperwork, could get under way even faster.

In an admirable effort to preserve important legal history, Chief Justice Hickman reveals an annual game played by those aboard the ship carrying justice to the outports. It went as follows:

As the ship neared the French possession of St. Pierre – which, as every schoolboy knows, is awash with cheap booze – the captain would say to the judge, "Your Lordship, I have just discovered a dreadful situation."

"What is that?" the judge would ask.

"Well, My Lord, even though we have been sailing only two days on a voyage that will take a month, we are out of potatoes."

"That is, indeed, a terrible situation," His Lordship would say, "and I hope it will never happen again."

"It won't, sir, believe me."

"But, in the meantime, we had better put into the nearest port and get a load of potatoes."

"Aye, aye, sir," the captain would reply.

The schooner would put into St. Pierre, where passengers and crew would force themselves to party for a day or so before sailing on to the nearby port of Grand Bank.

There was no courthouse in Grand Bank, so the judicial party, hangovers and all, headed for the place where court was traditionally held in that community – Temperance Hall, owned and operated by "The Sons of Temperance, Grand Division No. 9."

"I grew up in Grand Bank," Chief Justice Hickman says, "and though I'm too young to have sailed on the boat circuit, I have been in Temperance Hall many times and I can describe it in great detail from memory. I can also imagine how difficult it must have been to hold court in that room, what with all the distractions that one encountered there."

The walls of said room were plastered with drawings of John Barleycorn and posters that screamed out such sorrowful slogans as "Wine Is a Mocker" and "Strong Drink Is Raging" and "Look Not Upon the Wine When It Is Red."

John Pius Mulcahy had been practising law in St. John's, Newfoundland, for five years when he was appointed a magistrate. That was in 1937, when he was a tender twenty-nine years of age. He served on the bench for thirty-five years – in St. George's, Corner Brook, Bell Island, Gander, Goose Bay, and finally, for twenty-eight years, in St. John's.

When Mulcahy went on the bench, and for a very long time thereafter, he was one of only two magistrates in all of Newfoundland who'd studied and practised law. The other was Hugh O'Neill, who practised briefly, then served as a magistrate for forty-two years in St. John's before going back into practice in that city. Hugh's still practising there today, a decade after leaving the bench. Mulcahy and O'Neill also trained dozens of others to be magistrates.

Mulcahy was no stranger to bush-league justice. In his days in the outports there were few roads, and travel to and from court was usually by motorboat – a situation that still prevails in many remote parts of Newfoundland. Before Mulcahy brought his legal training into the hinterland, doctors often served as magistrates. In one case, in Corner Brook, a lawyer moved that the case against his client be dismissed. The doctor-magistrate looked out at the audience and said, "There's a motion on the floor. All in favour say aye."

"When I went to Bell Island in 1940," Mulcahy says, "I couldn't believe my eyes. The courthouse, which had been there since about 1890, was nearly falling down. It had been condemned for a long time, but Newfoundland was practically bankrupt in those days and the government hadn't gotten around to replacing it. The door to the magistrate's office was broken, and in the wintertime the snow would come through the cracks and collect in small drifts in the office. And in the courtroom, the oil paper on the ceiling was hanging down in strips. The customs people, the Newfoundland Constabulary, and the local police also had offices in that building, and we all used one outdoor toilet. There was a cubbyhole to put a prisoner in. I remember one prisoner who said, 'You wouldn't put a dog in there!' Fortunately, a new courthouse was erected a couple of years later."

Mulcahy often travelled by boat to completely isolated communities. There were no courtrooms in such places, and the magistrate would have to hear cases wherever he could.

"I once held court in a boxcar," Mulcahy says. "Another time, I heard cases on the beach to accommodate fishermen who had to get back to work as soon as possible. I've presided in kitchens, cloak rooms, living rooms, school basements. On one occasion, when I was trying a man in his living room, several local residents came to the front door and were let in by the man's wife. They walked past the living room, into the next room, and a few minutes later they left. That happened several times. A few witnesses who were waiting to testify also went into that room for a while, then came back into the living room to listen to some more of the case. I found out later that while I was holding court the lady of the house had been doing quite a bit of bootlegging in the next room."

After teaching school in Newfoundland for fifteen years, C. Maxwell Lane was appointed a magistrate in 1937. He was on the bench for fourteen years and then became a labour organizer and a politician, serving for eight years in Joey Smallwood's cabinet. Only three times in his judicial career in the Newfoundland outports did a lawyer appear in Lane's court – and very rarely was there an actual courtroom to hold court in. Lane, now eighty-two, says he usually presided in church halls, lodge halls, one-room schoolhouses, and living rooms. Many a time he held court at a fish stage, using the splitting table as a desk.

Outport justice can be pretty casual. A few years ago, Provincial Court Judge Gordon Seabright, accompanied by a policeman, was travelling along the south coast of Newfoundland in a motorboat. "We had twenty communities to visit," Seabright said recently. "We'd drop into each place and ask the local justice of the peace if there were any cases to be heard. If there were, I'd hear them that day. J.P.s aren't allowed to hear cases, you see. If there weren't any cases we'd move on to the next community and see how things were there.

"We went into a hamlet where there was a minor charge to be heard, but there was no place we could rent for a courtroom. The accused himself solved the problem. He said, 'You can come up to the house.' So we did. The officer opened court in the man's living room. I read the charge. The accused pleaded guilty. I imposed a twenty-five-dollar fine. The man paid it. We chatted for a while, then left. Everyone was so cordial."

And so it goes. North, south, east, west – wherever you might roam in this vast land, if you wander very far off the beaten path you're likely to run smack-dab into bush-league justice. And that ain't necessarily all bad news – not if you like laughs with your litigation – for the fact is that "the boonies" often spell F-U-N.

Sidney B. Simons spends much of his time labouring in his law office in downtown Vancouver, but he gets around a lot, too. "Slippery Sid," as he's affectionately known, is a member of the bars of both British Columbia and Alberta, and for a quarter of a century now he's been trying cases all over those two provinces. Sid's an excellent raconteur, and when he gets to telling legal stories you notice that many of his favourites are about tank towns – two in particular.

In the early 1960s Simons journeyed to Creston, British Columbia, to defend a criminal case. In Creston, which is near the Canada–U.S. border, just north of Idaho, the "courtroom" was a glorified broom closet at the back of the police station.

"Let me set the scene," Sid says. "There was a card table for the magistrate, and another card table was jammed up against it. That table was shared by the prosecutor, the court reporter, and me. There wasn't room in there for anyone else but a witness and the accused. Every bit of space was used up – I mean every bloody inch.

"The case was being heard by a lay magistrate – a fellow with no formal legal training – and since Creston's so close to the border he'd probably seen lots of 'Perry Mason' shows and that sort of thing on American television channels.

"Midway through the trial, when we were starting to feel claustrophobic, the prosecutor and I were arguing a point of law. The magistrate said, 'Just a minute! Just a minute! Will the attorneys please approach the bench?'

"There wasn't any room for us to *move*, for God's sake! The only way we could have 'approached the bench' was to lean forward! My opponent and I broke up. So did everyone else, except the guy on the 'bench.' "

"Slippery Sid" used to love going to court in Alexis Creek, British Columbia. "Ah, Alexis Creek!" he says. "That's where you'll find the genuine article – *real* bush-league justice!"

Alexis Creek is in the interior of B.C., about two hundred miles due north of Vancouver. Court used to be held in a room in the local hotel, dubbed "the Alexis Creek Hilton" by thirsty patrons, but because it was exceedingly difficult to get witnesses and other necessary parties out of the bar and into the courtroom, the seat of justice was moved to a room over a little log-cabin grocery store across the street from the pub.

"To compensate for this setback," Simons says, 'witnesses would each bring a case of beer to the new 'courthouse' and they'd polish it off while waiting in the hall to give evidence."

Just getting to Alexis Creek was an ordeal, "Slippery Sid" says. "Once I got to Williams Lake, I joined up with the judge, the prosecutor, and the court reporter, and we had to drive about fifty miles on very dusty gravel roads. When we got to Alexis Creek we were coated with dust and could hardly breathe or speak. You had to have something to wash away the dust.

"There was a lovely old judge who presided there. He *insisted* that we wash away the dust, but it had to be done in a hotel room, which he would rent, and we'd have to get the beer because it wouldn't look right for him to get it. Two or three bottles of beer were essential before we could go to the court and do anything. What a considerate man that judge was!"

Yes, indeed, life in the sticks can be vexing. Consider the sad case of Judge Jack Corey, of the County Court of Manitoba.

One frigid winter's morning, Judge Corey awoke in a tiny rural hotel and discovered that (a) he'd overslept and had only a few minutes to catch the train for the next town in his circuit, and (b) his false teeth were frozen in the water glass he'd placed them in the night before.

What to do? Unable to thaw his choppers in the short time available and unwilling to face the management without his teeth properly in place, His Honour slipped the glass into his pocket and dashed for the train without checking out of the hotel. With great chagrin, he later explained what had happened and settled his account with the innkeeper.

Late one morning a few years ago, Orillia, Ontario, lawyer Richard N. Clarke, Q.C., went into a dance hall in the nearby village of Brechin and sat down at a table. The dance hall was part of the premises of the local Royal Canadian Legion, but till later in the day if would function as a courtroom. Below the dance hall was another Legion facility called a bar. It wasn't functioning as a bar just then because it wasn't open yet. But in a few more minutes – at noon – it would start functioning as a bar again. And while it was so functioning, the dance hall would, of course, continue to function as a courtroom.

Mr. Clarke was not waiting for a drink. He had come to these premises to see if he could get a fellow off on a criminal charge. His case hadn't been called yet, so he just sat there and thought about his case a bit and just kind of glanced around the dance hall, uh, courtroom, every now and then.

About 12:15, the case that had been droning on for some time was concluded and the Crown Attorney called the next case, The Queen versus John Jones.

John Jones did not respond to the calling of his name, so the Crown Attorney fairly shouted it – "John Jones? John Jones?"

Still no answer.

"I think I can find him, Your Honour," said a man in the body of the court. "Give me a couple of minutes."

"All right," sighed the judge, drumming his fingers on the bench.

In two or three minutes the volunteer returned and announced, "Your Honour, he'll be up just as soon as he finishes his beer!"

In all of the cases chronicled in this chapter, no matter how "bush league" they might otherwise be, the participants and spectators were wearing some sort of clothing. The "bushiest" bush-league justice would be a trial in which everyone sat around in the altogether – reminiscent of the first case ever tried, God versus Adam and Eve.

Mr. Justice George L. Murray of the Supreme Court of British Columbia cannot tell us of any such case. But he comes close.

Back in the early 1960s, before he was appointed to the bench, George Murray prosecuted a great many Doukhobors – more accurately, members of the radical sect known as Sons of Freedom – on charges of arson and terrorism. The trials, which went on for six months, were held in the courthouse at Nelson, British Columbia.

The courthouse was not a nudist colony; it just looked like one. In case after case the defendants, and half the audience, observed the traditional Sons of Freedom protest – yanking rip cords, which immediately divested them of their duds. The authorities ignored this quaint practice; opposing it would have produced big problems that they didn't need. But it galled George Murray and other traditionalists, who just couldn't shake the idea that when folks get together in public places, dammit, they should wear clothes.

One day, in the dead of winter, George Murray had a brainwave. He told the RCMP officers in charge of security that, starting tomorrow, there'd be a new set-up in court. The Mounties were instructed to replace the wooden chairs with steel chairs. Not only that, but the new chairs were to be left out all night and put in place only moments before court began in the morning.

His Lordship chuckles when he recalls the scene – dozens of bare backs and bums coming into sudden contact with icy steel.

"What a sight!" he says. "Inside five minutes, everyone had their clothes back on."

It is probably the cheekiest thing George Murray has ever done.

15

Meanwhile, Back at the Office

Let's leave the courtroom for a spell and see how things are back at Headquarters. In other words, let's go to the office.

Even the busiest lawyers and judges spend gobs of time at the office. You don't think those brilliant cross-examinations and sparkling judgments just trip off the tongue, do you? Do you think witnesses are found under "W" in the yellow pages? Who do you think solves all those thorny legal problems and choreographs all those dazzling tactical manoeuvres—the Tooth Fairy? And where, pray tell, is most of this work done?

Anyone who watches "Perry Mason" knows that the office is the place where the hard slugging is done, the centre of operations where the facts are ferreted out and, slowly but surely, the case takes shape. Why, look at all the time Perry spends interviewing his obviously innocent client. Where does he usually do this? In the office. Look at all the conversations he has with Paul Drake and Della Street about how the case is coming along. Where do these talks take place? In the office. And even when Perry wins the case, does he take Paul and Della out for a victory drink? No, they go back to the office and chat about how the hell Perry knew whodunnit. You get the idea. Much of the time, the office is "*it*."

Now that doesn't mean that if we hole up in the office for a while everything will be deadly serious and we won't have any laughs. Oh, no. Sometimes the office can be a regular riot, what with lawyers and clients and secretaries making cracks that break you up. That eases the tension and leaves you feeling refreshed. The tension rebuilds, of course, but it won't be long before someone delivers a line that gives you that great feeling again. Clients are pretty good at that, but not always on purpose.

Some of the things that are said and done don't strike you as all that hilarious at the time. They seem funny *later*. I guess that's what James Thurber was getting at when he said that humour is "emotional chaos remembered in tranquillity."

When I think of those words, I automatically think of children – specifically, children who run amok in law offices.

I recall, not so fondly, the time a woman with four children in tow came to see me about a lawsuit. The two youngest squirmed in her arms while their brothers, about four and five years old, ran around the office knocking things over and "punching out" several shelves of law books. When their mother screamed at them to stop, they dived under my desk and untied my shoe laces.

Winnipeg lawyer Manly S. Rusen, a born comedian if ever there was one, has a hilarious routine in which he acts out the parts of all eight persons involved in a "drama" that took place in his office. A man and his wife came to sign documents and to get the details of their upcoming real-estate transaction. Naturally, for such an important occasion they brought along all five of their children.

"I have a nice clean office," Manly says with pride. "At least it was clean before those kids got a run at it. You should've seen them – dirty parkas, runny noses, fighting with each other all the time! They smeared their filthy hands over everything in sight, including my new wallpaper."

Manly cracks up his listeners as he jumps around the room, reliving the event. "Every time I said 'sign here' or told the couple anything about the deal, the mother would smack the kids – even the ones who hadn't done anything. It was trauma, man, pure trauma! And when they finally left the mother said, 'Nice office you've got here!' "

Saskatoon lawyer Grant M. Currie sends this dispatch from the battlefront: "I once was interviewing a lady who had brought along her two small boys. While she talked, oblivious to her children's antics, I watched the older boy dig far into his nose and pull out the kind of thing you'd expect him to find there.

"The younger boy, just old enough to lean up against the chair, was eyeing this. Then, as though it had happened many times before, the younger boy opened his mouth to receive the offering that his brother carefully placed there. When I came to, the boys had moved on to gnawing the furniture and their mother was still talking."

Gerald A. Dust, a lawyer in Orleans, Ontario, writes: "I have a large real-estate practice. My office is located in a suburb with a large population of young families. I frequently sign up real-estate deals with children in my office.

"In the summer of 1986 a young mother came in to review and sign documents on a mortgage transaction. She brought her three-year-old son with her. Many of the children who visit our office enjoy our toy box. His eyes never left me once he entered the office, and he chose to sit in a chair against the back wall, as far away from me as he could get. Throughout the half-hour interview he stared at me very solemnly.

"I like children and pride myself on my ability to get them to open up. I don't want them going away with the impression that lawyers are boring. Despite my best efforts, I was unable to get either a word or a smile out of this young fellow.

"Finally, the mortgage was signed and the mother had no more questions. At his mother's invitation, the little boy was quick to jump off the chair and head for the door. As he grabbed his mother's hand and left my office, I heard him say, 'No needle today, Mommy?'"

Frank Maczko, Q.C., secretary of the Law Society of British Columbia, recently sent me a batch of good stories. Here's one of them, in Frank's own words:

"While I was the director of the Legal Aid Society of B.C., Fred Reagh, then a staff lawyer at Legal Aid, interviewed a client who was applying for legal aid on a drug charge. Fred was going to act for him on a guilty plea. On the day of the trial the accused did not show up. The next day, Fred received a phone call.

"Fred described the fellow as so drugged up that he was barely aware of his surroundings and had an emaciated look and 'snakes' on his arms (snakes are dark lines made by repeated use of the needle).

"On the day he did not show up for the court the accused came to the office later in the day and Fred, feeling sorry for him, offered to take him out for some food, which the fellow turned down.

"Then Fred offered to buy him a cup of coffee. The accused said, 'I don't drink coffee.'

"When Fred asked why not, the accused responded, 'Oh, it's got caffeine in it. That's bad for your health.'"

Another yarn from Maczko's memoirs:

"A fellow about sixty-five years old came to see me with his brother, who was a couple of years younger. They wanted to have their father, who was almost ninety years old, declared incompetent under the Patients Estate Act. The two brothers were convinced that he was going to fritter away his entire estate. They based this on the fact that he was bringing prostitutes in for the night, was spending his money lavishly on them while carrying on in debauchery and drinking, and, God forbid, sexual intercourse.

"I told the two gentlemen that they would have to get two doctors to sign affidavits stating that the old man was not capable of managing his affairs or himself. They went off to arrange the evidence, and I heard nothing from them for a couple of months. They then phoned me and asked me how the case was going. I told them that I had not heard from even one doctor, let alone two.

"They told me that they had spoken to their father's doctor, who had seen the 'patient,' and the doctor assured them that he would be contacting me. I got the name of the doctor and wrote to him directly. The doctor replied, saying the evidence of the gentleman's ability to look after his affairs was demonstrated by the very activity complained about.

"I phoned the doctor and, after a rather frank conversation, the doctor said: 'The old fart will probably drink and screw himself to death, but that's hardly evidence of incapacity.' "

Newmarket, Ontario, lawyer Daniel W. Monteith checks in with this tail, er, tale: "My client had a record of at least forearm-length and was facing charges of theft, possession of stolen property, assault, and two counts of possession of narcotics. We somehow persuaded the Crown to drop all but two of the charges and obtained a sentence of modest fines on both convictions.

"My secretary was making her usual semimonthly telephone calls to collect delinquent accounts, and a call was made to this fellow. There had been a small balance outstanding on his account for several weeks. My secretary suggested to my client's girlfriend, who had answered the call, that her boyfriend should be grateful that we got him off and gladly pay up. Her immediate reply was, 'Well, I get him off all the time, and he's never paid me yet.' "

The phone rang in a Hamilton law office.

"How's my husband's suit coming along?" the caller asked the secretary who answered the phone.

"Please give me your name and number," the secretary replied. "I'll find out and call you back."

The secretary, a rookie, had started her career that week. She wasn't at all familiar with the firm's files, and after a thorough but unsuccessful search, she phoned the lady back.

"Could you give me some specific information regarding the suit?" she asked.

"It's blue," the woman said testily, then added: "Isn't this ABC Cleaners?"

The phone rang in the office of the Law Reform Commission of Canada.

"I wish to speak to the president of the Law Reform Commission," a woman announced.

"I'm sorry, he's not in," replied a secretary. "Is there anything I can do for you?"

"Just tell him I know what you're up to over there."

"What are we up to?"

"Don't pretend you don't know."

"Honestly, I don't know what you mean."

"Not just you – the whole legal profession. I know all about it, and you're not going to get away with it. We have ways of protecting ourselves against people like you."

"What do you mean?"

"The isotopes. You know. We're being bombarded day and night by radioactive isotopes, by the legal profession. It's all being handled by the Law Reform Commission, but you won't get away with it. Tell *that* to your president!"

Click!

Later the secretary relayed the message to the president, Mr. Justice Allen M. Linden, of the Supreme Court of Ontario.

"How did she find out about this?" His Lordship asked. "We thought nobody knew."

The phone rang, again, in the office of the Law Reform Commission of Canada.

"Could you tell me how you go about changing the laws?" a woman asked.

"Well," said a secretary, "the Law Reform Commission influences law reform in many ways. We develop recommendations, sponsor legal research, and hope that our ideas will have an effect on the various levels of the legal system. We put out reports, working papers, study papers. We publish articles. We do a lot of things. Our ideas go to Parliament for their consideration . . ."

"Boy, it sounds complicated!"

"Well, it is, but it's a job that needs doing."

"So if there's a law that needs changing, we let you know about it?"

"Well, what law did you have in mind?"

"Our bridge club wants to change its regulations and I saw your name in the phone book . . ."

The phone rang in a law office in Courtenay, British Columbia:

Calgary legal secretary Jennifer M. Foy writes: "One of the secretaries where I work was busy taking off her coat and boots after arriving at the office. Her boss had been looking for her frantically for a while, and when he finally saw her he said exuberantly, 'When you get your clothes off, come in for some dictation.' "

Mr. Justice Melvin E. Shannon of the Court of Queen's Bench of Alberta reports: "Most of the judges at the courthouse in Calgary have their offices on the ninth floor. A number of orderlies work at the reception desk on that floor, and lawyers who want to see a judge must arrange to do so through an orderly. A young lawyer told me that on one occasion she arrived at the ninth floor and asked the orderly if she could see a certain judge. The orderly said that he would make inquiries and let her know. He disappeared through the door leading to the judges' offices and returned within a minute. His response was: 'He says to tell you that he's in Edmonton.' "

Robert B. McGee, Q.C., of Toronto tells a gripping tale of drama in a law office.

In the 1960s, Toronto lawyer Hugh Locke (now Judge Locke) practised mostly family law, and his partner, David G. Humphrey (now Judge Humphrey), specialized in criminal law. One day a distraught woman who was suing her husband for divorce bawled her eyes out while she waited for Locke to return from court. Hugh was held up for quite some time, and when the woman started wailing a concerned secretary stepped into Humphrey's office and asked him if he'd try to settle her down.

"I'll be glad to," Dave replied. "Send the poor lady in."

One of Humphrey's clients had recently given him a revolver and asked him to surrender it to the police. Dave hadn't gotten around to it yet.

While Locke's sobbing client was telling Humphrey what a complete and utter rat her husband was, Humphrey opened a desk drawer, pulled out the gun, loaded it, and then slipped it into his pocket. Immediately, the woman stopped crying.

"What are you doing?' she asked with alarm.

"What's his address?" Humphrey asked.

She told him.

Humphrey stood up and headed for the door.

"Where are you going?"

"Out to kill him."

"What?"

"You came to us for help and we're going to help you. I'm going to go and kill the bastard!"

"Oh, my God, don't do that!"

"I thought you hated him."

"I do, but not *that* much!"

"Well, all right," Dave said with a chuckle. "We'll talk instead."

"It worked," said Bob McGee. "Dave eventually calmed her down and she left the office quite happy."

Cornwall, Ontario, lawyer Thomas R. Swabey tells a story about another close call.

In the 1970s, when Tom was a member of the Provincial Court (Criminal Division) in Ottawa, anyone in the nation's capital who planned to commit matrimony in a setting other than a church or synagogue had to have the ceremony performed by a judge. Family Court judges and County Court judges flatly refused to oblige. The chore – and it was so regarded – fell to the judges of the Criminal Division of the Provincial Court. Most of the marriage ceremonies were performed in court – a *criminal* court. An inauspicious way to launch a marriage, some said.

"We Provincial Court judges used to joke that we handed out more life sentences in a week than most Supreme Court judges did in a whole career," says Swabey.

As the day of the official opening of the new National Arts Centre drew nigh, a certain VIP became increasingly concerned. The Governor General of Canada was throwing a gala reception to mark the big event, and the VIP had an invitation. The problem was that he was living with a woman he intended to marry when his pending divorce became final, but protocol prevented an invitation being extended to a "common-law spouse." Unless the divorce came through in time for the couple to be married, only the man would be attending the regal "do."

It was nip and tuck, but the divorce was finalized a very few days before the grand opening. Immediately, the VIP's lawyer contacted the administrator of the Provincial Court (Criminal Division) in Ottawa and started lining up a wedding ceremony.

To comply with provincial law regarding waiting periods and other formalities, Saturday was the only day the couple could be wed and still attend the festivities together. Saturday was also the day of the opening. However, the Provincial Court was closed on Saturday. The court administrator prevailed upon Judge Tom Swabey to come into his office on Saturday and unite the couple in the bonds of holy matrimony.

Accompanied by a large entourage of friends, the bride and groom arrived a few minutes before the ceremony was scheduled to start. They must have been in a hell of a hurry, because the bride's bouquet consisted of a bundle of rhubarb.

While Judge Swabey waited in his office, the administrator quickly obtained pertinent details and, with equal haste, wrote them in the wedding register. Everyone then trooped into the office, and the administrator handed the wedding register to Judge Swabey. In performing the ceremony, he'd read aloud the information recorded in the register.

"I had a sixty-to-ninety-second ceremony, designed to observe the requirements of the Marriage Act and nothing more," Tom Swabey recalled. "As I was about to pronounce the couple man and wife, one of the bridesmaids raised her hand, as if she were a school-girl asking to leave the room. I stopped in mid-sentence.

"She said, 'Excuse me, Your Honour, but you're about to marry the groom to *me*!' "

Swabey soon discovered that the court administrator had written the wrong name in the space reserved for "bride" when preparing the wedding register.

"Everyone had a good laugh and I then back-tracked, got the names straight, and married the right persons," Swabey said. "They all left my office quite happy."

A close call of a different sort occurred in the Legal Aid office in Walkerton, Ontario, several years ago. Secretary Sheila Stephenson tells the story: "A very large woman came in to apply for legal aid. She sat down in the waiting room, and when I was able to see her I said, 'If you'll come over here I'll take your application.' She got up to come toward me, and the chair came with her. She was hopelessly stuck! I said I'd help if I could. Little did I know what I was in for!

"After ten to fifteen minutes of pushing and pulling, I gave up. I couldn't free her, no matter how hard I tried. I phoned next door to a furniture store and one of the salesmen came running. He thought the situation was hilarious, but he couldn't get her out of the chair, either. It was a hot summer's day and the woman was sweating like a – well, like a stuck pig. The smell was overpowering.

"After several more minutes of struggle, to no avail, I suggested that the woman bend over and hold on to my desk. She did, and the salesman and I pushed and pried until we were finally able to loosen one side of the chair from the woman. By twisting and turning the chair, over and over again, and by pushing rolls of fat out of the way, we were finally able to free the rest of her. The salesman left, laughing his head off, and I interviewed the sweating, panting, smelly applicant for the next half hour. She stood the whole time. I wonder why?"

Nanaimo, British Columbia, lawyer Earl A. Bamford had a close call with some valuable clients who came to see him in his office. For a while he thought he'd lost them. Here's Earl:

"Recently I was appointed as counsel for a local Indian band to aid them in financing the construction and operation of a pleasure-craft marina costing approximately $550,000.

"I told them my fees for general time and consultation were $110 per hour and that financial-security documentation was usually one-quarter to one-half of one percent of the amount borrowed.

"One of the band council members looked me straight in the eye and asked, 'Would you consider taking back some of the coloured beads?' "

In thirty years of practice, Toronto lawyer Garry K. Braund, Q.C., has had countless clients. But none can compare with a Neanderthal fellow he called "Romeo." Garry tagged him with that moniker because of his knowledge – carnal, that is – of a wide variety of critters. Romeo passed on a few years ago, and his erstwhile counsel feels it's about time folks were given some insight into just how wacky some clients are. So here, in a nutshell, is the story of a nut called Romeo.

Romeo was a six-foot-two, three-hundred-pound lout, fortyish in age, who fell in love with a sixty-five-year-old bootlegger named Hazel. Garry Braund represented Romeo on several impaired-driving charges. In one case the accused drove stark naked on Toronto's Don Valley Parkway. In another, he smashed, fully clothed, into a train. In still another case Romeo beat the living hell out of his brother but avoided jail when Braund produced a bond in which his client promised never to do that sort of thing again.

"The lovers pooled their money and bought a two-hundred-acre farm several miles from Toronto," Braund reports. "Romeo needed animals, so he took Hazel in his second-hand, four-door Lincoln to an animal auction in Stouffville. Romeo was drunk and waved his hand in the air. Down came the gavel, and Romeo had bought a sow and her litter of pigs. Hazel told me that it was no problem putting the pigs in the front seat, but several hundred people were greatly amused as Romeo pulled and shoved the sow into the comfort of the rear seat. Then away they went to their new farm.

"Hazel would often phone me at the office to tell me that her man was having sexual encounters with the cattle, horses, geese, turkeys, and ducks. That's when I first realized the true meaning of the expression 'barnyard Romeo,' and that's when I dubbed him Romeo."

On one occasion, Hazel phoned to say that her drunken Romeo had been bringing a horse into the living room on a regular basis.

"So what, Hazel?" Braund remarked. "Nothing that fellow does should surprise you."

"Oh, I know," Hazel replied, "but the horse isn't housebroken. I'm really afraid of Romeo when he's drinking. What do you think I should do to get away from him now and then?"

"Get a magazine and go to the outhouse," her counsel advised.

"I tried that," Hazel replied, "but when I was in there with the door locked, Romeo took the front-end loader and lifted the outhouse in the air and drove all around the fields. I kept yelling, 'Put me down!' Put me down!' and he finally did."

Even though Romeo had inherited a large chunk of money, he was indifferent about going to Braund's office to sign papers that would make his new-found wealth come true. Braund had to leave his office and go see Romeo at the filthy, foul-smelling shack he called home.

"I went into the woodshed through stacks of boxes and then into the kitchen, which reeked of human and animal stench," Braund recalls. "The kitchen had a path through the filth. There, sitting at a table, was Romeo. At his side was Hazel. On the table was a forty-ounce bottle of rye, and beside the table were two large cases of beer.

"Romeo roared like an ape when he saw me. He always did that. That was his way of saying hello. I sat down to get the signatures I needed. Romeo was swigging straight from the rye bottle and chasing it with beer. He signed a couple of times and then threw a beer bottle at the wall. One more signature out of the way. He then got up, staggered over to the screen door, and urinated through the screen. Outside, on an old table, some large geese flapped their wings and honked as they watched their barnyard Romeo empty his bladder. Romeo lurched back to the table, and when he'd affixed his signature to the papers a few more times I bid them a fond adieu."

There were some other papers to sign on another occasion, and this time Romeo *did* make it into the office.

"He had a rooster inside his jacket," Braund recalls, "and he was feeding it beer from a plastic cup. I invited Romeo and his feathered friend into my office. Romeo removed an oatmeal cookie from his pocket, and the rooster kept pecking at the cookie and slurping beer from the cup.

"Suddenly, to my dismay, the rooster dropped a large 'bouquet' from under his tail onto my shiny walnut desk. When Romeo had gone I showed my secretary the large deposit on the desk, and she made a remark that is *so* true. 'You know,' she said, 'lawyers have to take a lot of shit from their clients.' "

16

Potpourri

Anyone who's run afoul of the law would be well advised to heed the words of the old saying, "He who acts as his own lawyer has a fool for a client."

Robert J. Lane, a lawyer in Shellbrook, Saskatchewan, provides proof positive that truer words were never spoken. Bob sent me a court-certified transcript of the arraignment–in Provincial Court in Prince Albert–of a fellow who represented himself on a charge of breaking and entering.

After the charge had been read to the accused, the court clerk informed him that he could elect to be tried in that court or in the Court of Queen's Bench, and then the judge explained this to him. We pick it up from there:

THE COURT: Do you understand it now, or would you like further explanation?

ACCUSED: I understand it.

THE COURT: Do you feel that you're prepared to elect and plead today, or do you want me to adjourn it so that you can take advice?

ACCUSED: I'll take it.

THE COURT: You want to elect today? Who do you elect?

ACCUSED: You.

THE COURT: And how do you plead, guilty or not guilty?

ACCUSED: I plead not guilty.

THE COURT (to the prosecutor): How many Crown witnesses will there be?

ACCUSED: Only one–the one I broke into the store with.

In another western case, a chap who acted for himself in fighting a robbery charge asked the man who'd been robbed: "Could you see my face clearly when I handed you the note?"

A judge who was slightly hard of hearing presided at the trial of a man accused of a serious offence. The evidence against the accused was overwhelming and his case was clearly hopeless, but he insisted on supplementing the speech of his counsel by delivering one of his own.

"I've never been in trouble before," the instant lawyer told the court, "and there are a number of matters I feel I've got to clear up for the sake of my good reputation."

The accused spoke rapidly and excitedly, but he was understandable for the first few minutes of his address. Then he picked up speed, and from then on the judge had a devil of a time comprehending what he was saying. Finally, overcome by emotion and the novelty of his task, the man became incoherent.

"Hold it!" said the judge, who'd been trying to jot down the main points of argument. "What was your last sentence?"

"Seven years," said the accused.

Another man who acted on his own behalf presented evidence that he felt would prove he was a split personality. The judge rejected the pitch and added, "Both of you will have to go to prison for eighteen months."

Frank Maczko, Q.C., secretary of the Law Society of British Columbia, recalls a case he was involved in when he was in practice. "I was interviewing a fellow at the B.C. Penitentiary, where he was doing eight years on a conviction for robbery," Frank writes. "He wanted to appeal his sentence. After reviewing his record I told him that there was virtually no chance of success. I told him that his best chance was to do his own appeal.

"I suggested he appear on his own, look real sorry, and promise never to do it again. The court would give him a long lecture, I said, and might knock off a couple of years in return for the lecture. He stared at me for about thirty seconds and then said, 'Ah, fuck it, I'd rather do my time!' "

Recalling his days in practice. Mr. Justice George L. Murray of the Supreme Court of British Columbia writes: "The late Nick Mussallem acted for a couple of bookmakers who had been fined one thousand dollars. He had not received his fee, so he took an appeal to the Court of Appeal, hoping to get his fee out of a reduced fine. When Chief Justice Davie called on me to present the Crown's position, he asked me to relate the amounts of the fines in recent cases.

"I told the court that the last case I was aware of was one where an elderly couple had had a fine of one thousand dollars reduced to five hundred dollars because of their unusual personal presentation of their appeal. This presentation consisted simply of standing at the lectern and breaking into tears.

"At this point, Mussallem tugged on my gown and said, 'Tell them that I, too, will cry if necessary.' I did as instructed. The fine was reduced. Mussallem got his fee, and everybody went home happy."

Mr. Justice Murray also reminisces about a conspiracy-to-defraud case he once prosecuted: "George Frederick Caldough, on his second trial before Mr. Justice Maclean and a jury, addressed the jury at great length in his own defence, and in his address he quoted at length from most of the great philosophers, including Aristotle, Sophocles, and Voltaire.

"It was a very scholarly address, and when Mr. Justice Maclean came to charge the jury he gave illustrations of the law of conspiracy. He said something to this effect: 'Suppose two policemen are hidden in the hayloft of a barn and they hear two men plotting below. One man says to the other, "Let's get together and steal Farmer Brown's cow," and the other man says, "Agreed" and the two men go out to steal Farmer Brown's cow but are apprehended before they succeed in stealing the cow from Farmer Brown – they are still guilty of conspiracy.'

"Both Caldough and his co-conspirator Smith were convicted. As they were being led down to the cells Smith turned to Caldough and said, 'Goddamn it, George, you spent all your time talking to that jury about Aristotle, Sophocles, and Voltaire. The judge spent *his* time talking to them about Farmer Brown's cow. It's no damn wonder we're going down these stairs now!' "

A few months later, Murray received a homemade Christmas card from Caldough in the penitentiary. All it said was, "Let joy be *unconfined!*"

Sudbury lawyer Robert Del Frate tells a story of an elderly man who represented himself on four criminal charges. He had a long record, and the judge said he had no alternative but to sentence the man to ten years in prison.

"But, Your Honour," the man protested, "I'm seventy-three years old! I'll never make it!"

"Well," said the kindly judge, "do the best you can."

From time to time, persons who've been convicted and are about to be sentenced somehow manage to come up with a funny remark. Provincial Court Judge G. Hughes Randall of Halifax writes: "In 1985, Moosehead Breweries, brewers of a lager called Alpine, ran a TV commercial in the Maritimes that depicted a man appearing before a Spanish firing squad. When asked by the captain in charge if there were any last requests prior to being shot, the man replied, 'An Alpine would go down good at a time like this.'

"In the fall of 1985, three young men appeared before a judge in Pictou County, Nova Scotia, for sentencing on an armed-robbery charge. Before sentencing, the judge asked all three accused if they had anything to say before sentence. One of them replied, 'An Alpine would go down good at a time like this.' "

A few years ago, Halifax *Chronicle-Herald* reporter Dean Jobb covered the trial of a man charged with attempted break and enter. In their addresses to the judge, the prosecutor and the defence lawyer spoke about whether or not the accused should be incarcerated. The man in the dock winced every time he heard the word.

"Is there anything you wish to say before I pass sentence?" Judge Peter O'Hearn asked the accused.

"Yes, Your Honour," he replied. "I know I done wrong, and I know I've got to pay for it, but I really think that castration would do me more harm than good."

Ottawa lawyer Roydon J. Kealey, Q.C., was in court one day and heard the following exchange:

JUDGE: Mr. Maloney, you've been found guilty of the charge brought against you. Is there anything you wish to say before I impose the sentence of the court?
ACCUSED: Yeah, there sure is!
JUDGE: What do you want to say, Mr. Maloney?
ACCUSED: My name's Murphy!

Crown Attorney Brian Farmer, of Walkerton, Ontario, recalls a case he prosecuted in London several years ago. A young man pleaded guilty to a shoplifting charge and was lectured sternly by Provincial Court Judge J. M. Seneshen.

"The next time you come before me you're going to go to jail," His Honour warned, "so you'd better bring your toothbrush and a six-month supply of toothpaste!"

The culprit looked up at the judge and quipped, "Yeah, and a jar of Vaseline!"

Crown Attorney John S. Alexander, Q.C., of Barrie, Ontario, relates the sad story of a man whose bladder nearly burst. A farmer bringing produce into the town of Goderich found himself travelling the wrong way on a one-way street. Traffic was congested, and the farmer had no opportunity to exit or turn around. To make matters worse, he had an excruciating need to pee. When he couldn't stand it any longer he jumped out of his truck, and right then and there obtained blessed relief.

A nearby policeman saw this and charged the farmer with indecent exposure. The accused pleaded not guilty, but after hearing the evidence the judge reluctantly concluded that the charge had been proven. "However," he added, "I'm going to make the fine extremely light – fifteen dollars, and three dollars costs."

The farmer walked to the front of the courtroom, tossed a twenty-dollar bill on the clerk's desk, and turned to leave.

"Hold it," said the judge, "You've got two dollars coming to you."

"Keep the change, Your Honour," the man declared. "I'll be back in town again someday and I may want to fart!"

Garry K. Braund, Q.C., of Toronto recalls a case in which he acted for two men charged with the same offence.

"What's your address?" the court clerk asked one of the accused.

"No fixed address," the man replied.

"And what's *your* address?" the clerk asked the co-accused.

"Same address," came the reply.

Cornwall, Ontario, lawyer Thomas R. Swabey, a former judge of the Provincial Court (Criminal Division) in Ottawa, tells of an impaired-driving case heard by his colleague, Judge Livius Sherwood, back in the days before suspects had to submit to the breathalyzer machine. "It was a marginal case," Tom said. "If defence counsel had quit after the Crown's evidence was in and said 'There's no case to meet,' the judge would have thrown the case out."

But the defence lawyer, a raw rookie, handled things quite differently. "I'm very upset about the unfair way the Crown has conducted its case," he told Judge Sherwood. "Obviously the Crown hasn't called everyone who saw the accused from the time of his arrest. My client was put into jail after he was arrested, and the Crown hasn't called the desk sergeant or the man who put him in the cells."

"I don't want to be unfair, Your Honour," said the Crown Attorney. "If you give me a brief adjournment, I'll see if I can find the officer who put the accused in jail." The request was granted.

The Crown Attorney strolled next door to the police station, and five minutes later he returned with the man who'd locked up the accused. The officer took the stand.

"I have no questions," the Crown Attorney told the court.

The young defence lawyer rose eagerly to his feet and waded into the witness.

"You saw my client when he was put into the cells?"

"Yes."

"Did my client say anything when he was put into the cells?"

The witness paused a moment or two, pondering the question.

"Not at first," he said, "but a while later he was making some noise, so I went back to see him. He looked at me through the bars and said, 'If I wasn't so stone drunk, I'd swear I was in jail!' "

There are plenty of stories about jurors. Let's consider a few.

William R. Poole, Q.C., is an outstanding criminal lawyer in London, Ontario. In a career that stretches back to 1949, he's defended nearly a hundred persons charged with murder. This yarn has to do with his very first murder case.

The accused, a former commando, lived in a trailer with his common-law wife and twelve-year-old son. One day, when he was drunk, he shot the woman dead as she sat near the door of the trailer. Poole interviewed the son and learned that whenever the accused had a snootful he got out his shotgun and fired through the open door of the trailer. "Dad often missed," the lad told Poole, pointing to a great many patched holes in the vicinity of the door. Poole counted twenty-four such patch-jobs, and the boy said there would have been at least a dozen other times that his father had fired and not hit something inside.

For five days, witness after witness testified for the Crown – policemen, ballistic experts, scientists from the crime lab – and Bill Poole refrained from asking a single question of any of these people. There was method in his madness: The only person who could offer any meaningful evidence was the accused's son. He was Poole's only witness, and Poole had to wait for the opportunity to put him on the stand.

When the Crown had completed its case, Poole called the youngster, who told the judge and jury all about his father's three-dozen shooting sprees. In his address to the jury, Poole said it was unfortunate that the woman was sitting near the door when the accused got the urge to shoot, but it was obvious that the man had had no intention of shooting her. "If you conclude that he intended to kill her," he told the jurors, "then you would also have to conclude that he attempted murder on thirty-five previous occasions. And if this is so, why did the woman continue to sit near the door when my client had been drinking? She obviously didn't think he wanted to kill her."

The trial judge, Mr. Justice Dan Kelly, called it "a brilliant defence," and the jury convicted the man of the lesser charge of manslaughter – which, of course, meant that he wouldn't be hanged. The young lawyer was extremely proud of himself.

In those distant days it was permissible for a lawyer to speak to members of the jury, once the case was over, and learn what he could about what impressed them and what turned them off. It was a highly educational experience, and most counsel grabbed every opportunity they could to learn in this fashion.

Shortly after the trial, Bill Poole saw the foreman and several members of the jury going into a pub. He went in, too, and engaged them in conversation.

"What did you think of my argument?" Poole proudly asked the foreman.

"Huh?"

"You know, my argument about not intending to kill."

He repeated the argument that had so impressed the judge. It didn't impress the former jurors.

"Why did you let my client off on the murder charger?" Poole inquired.

"Oh, it doesn't matter," the foreman said vaguely.

"Of course it does!" Poole said, obviously piqued. "This is my first case. I want to learn."

"Well, all right, Mister," snapped the foreman. "You didn't do anything for your client for five whole days. The Crown Attorney had all those witnesses, and you didn't even ask them *one* question!"

"Yes, but – "

"By the end of the fourth day we'd decided that if you weren't going to help this poor vet, *we were!*"

David Muise, a lawyer in Sydney, Nova Scotia, loves to tell of a jury case that was tried down the road in Baddeck. The jurors were having trouble reaching a decision, so they trooped back into court for further instructions from the judge. Everyone in court thought the jurors were returning to announce the big news.

"Members of the jury, have you reached a verdict?" the judge inquired.

The foreman of the jury stood and said, "Well, Your Honour, some of us thinks he done it and some of us thinks he never done it. Myself, I think he's innocent and should get off with a light sentence."

In 1985, at the opening of a session of the Supreme Court of Ontario at Stratford, Mr. Justice Joseph Potts told the jury panel it was extremely important that jurors be able to hear well. He asked if any of the potential jurors had any difficulty in that regard. One of them said she did. Thanks to court reporter Gail McGilvray, we have a transcript:

POTENTIAL JUROR: I am hard of hearing in one ear, but if they talk loud it's all right. I might have to ask them to repeat something.

HIS LORDSHIP: I think if that is the case we better not take a chance. You will be excused. You name, ma'am?

POTENTIAL JUROR: No, I don't have a hearing aid at home.

HIS LORDSHIP: I guess I made the right decision there. You are excused.

POTENTIAL JUROR: Pardon?

Also in 1985, at London, Ontario, Gail McGilvray reported a sexual-assault case in which evidence disclosed that the accused had had intercourse with the complainant four times in an hour-and-a-half to two hours. Defence counsel advised the court that he wouldn't be calling any evidence, and the case was adjourned until the next day for the lawyers' jury addresses and the judge's charge to the jury.

As the jury was leaving the courthouse, Gail walked behind two of the jurors. She couldn't help hearing the following exchange:

FEMALE JUROR: I'm disappointed the accused isn't going to give evidence.

MALE JUROR: Me, too. I wouldn't mind even asking him a few questions — number one, what the hell does he eat?

Ottawa lawyer Daniel H. McGuire once defended a man on a charge of raping a young woman. "There were eleven men and one woman on the jury," Danny reports. "I didn't want the woman, but I'd used up all my challenges and I was stuck with her."

In his address to the jury McGuire said, "The complainant says that my client raped her in the laneway and she ran up the laneway, screaming, but no one heard her, and then she stopped and waited for my client to catch up with her and walk her home."

What followed was like something out of "Perry Mason."

The complainant leaped to her feet and screamed, "That's not true! That's a lie!"

"It *is* true," yelled the woman juror that McGuire had wanted to dump, "and your mother should have spanked your ass!"

Provincial Court Judge R. N. Conroy of Saskatoon tells of a jury trial that took place years ago in Battleford:

A farmer was charged with bestiality after he became amorous with one of his cows. The chief Crown witness, the hired man, testified that he saw his boss place a milk stool behind the cow and then stand on same in preparation for the act. Moments later, the witness said, the cow kicked the stool over and the farmer fell to the floor of the barn.

A farmer in the jury box slapped his knee and exclaimed, "They'll do that every time!"

For some unexplained reason there's always a lively interest in our next subject – adultery. District Court Judge James A. Clare of Barrie, Ontario, is our first narrator. He writes:

"While in practice I did little matrimonial work, but I remember an occasion when a lady came in and told me she wanted me to act for her in a divorce action. I asked her if she was living with her husband, and she said she had left her husband and her girlfriend Gladys had taken her and her children into her home and had been wonderful to them. She went on at some length to praise her friend Gladys.

"I then asked about the ground for divorce, which she said was adultery. I explained that detailed evidence would be required to prove the adultery and asked what evidence she had as to adultery and did she have any witnesses who could testify as to the adultery. She replied, 'There's no problem about getting evidence of his adultery because my girlfriend Gladys slept with him many times.' "

Calgary lawyer Robert Densmore writes: "My late mentor, good friend, and partner, Judge Bill Sellar, would have enjoyed your book. He often traded stories with Mr. Justice Jimmy Cairns and Mr. Justice Harold Riley. Originally an Easterner, but finally a confirmed and dedicated Westerner, he loved people and was able to laugh with them and at himself. Above all, he enjoyed a good story.

"One of his favourites, from my early memories of him, concerned a rather distraught female client who sought his counsel. She told him of her husband's shortcomings – he was never home, he drank too much, he was abusive. In short, she wanted a divorce. Her husband had been running around with other women and committing adultery. 'In fact,' she said, 'he has been committing so much adultery that I don't even think that our last three kids are his!' "

William Church, Q.C., of Orangeville, Ontario, tells of a case he was involved in. A ten-year-old boy was being questioned as to how he knew that his father and his father's new girlfriend slept together. "That's easy," the boy replied. "Me and my brothers went into their bedroom every morning and woke them up."

Roger Carter, a professor of law at the University of Saskatchewan, recalls a matrimonial case in which Roy Romanow, Q.C., later attorney general of the province, asked a witness, "Isn't it a fact that you are living in adultery?"

"Oh, no! Oh, no!" the man replied. "I live on a farm near Kindersley."

In another case – one of my favorites – the lawyer for the plaintiff asked the respondent, "Isn't it true that on the night of June 11th, in an orchard at (giving exact location), you had relations with the co-respondent on the back of his motorcycle?"

There was complete silence for nearly three minutes. Then the woman replied, "What was that date again?"

James B. Chadwick, Q.C., of Ottawa did a lot of agency work for Newfoundland lawyers back in the days (before 1968) when the only way people from that province could obtain a divorce was to air their dirty linen before a special committee of the Canadian Senate.

In one unforgettable case Jim handled, the husband left his wife, the petitioner, and phoned her later to say, "We've got to get a divorce."

"How do we do that?" his wife inquired, and hubbie replied, "You go out and get laid."

"I said okay," the petitioner testified, "so I went out to the air base at Argentia and I met this fellow from the Phillipines who was in the American navy."

"What did you say to him?" Chadwick asked.

"I said, 'You want to get laid?' "

"What did he say?"

"He said, 'Gee. Sure.' He was delighted."

"Did you go somewhere with him?"

"We went to my house."

"What happened there?"

"We sat in the living room. He got me once in the living room."

"Are you saying you had sexual intercourse?" Chadwick asked.

"Huh?"

"Did you have a sexual relationship?"

"Huh?"

The divorce commissioner told Chadwick, "Put it to her plainly."

"Did he screw you?"

"Oh, Lord Jesus, yes! He screwed me once there, once on the back stairs, and once upstairs in the bedroom!"

Keith E. Eaton, Q.C., of Chester Basin, Nova Scotia, recalls a memorable Bluenose divorce case: "Chief Justice James Lorimer Ilsley, who as a hard-shelled Baptist was tough on divorces under the old adultery law, asked a witness how she knew what happened in a hotel room when she was in the corridor outside. She replied, 'All I know is he had a hard-on before he went in and it was gone when he came out.' The divorce was granted."

When he was a young lawyer in the Department of Justice in Ottawa, the same Keith Eaton was sent to Sydney, Nova Scotia, to testify in an action being heard there by an elderly judge of the Exchequer Court of Canada.

"I gave very technical evidence to support the technical defence that the Crown had entered in the lawsuit," Eaton says. "The judge got my name down as 'Egan,' but we didn't bother correcting him.

"Following a lobster-and-beer party that night, Ed Cragg, the Halifax lawyer acting for the Crown, called me to say he had 'the runs' and couldn't argue the case. I said that I was disqualified because I had given evidence. Ed said it would be all right if everyone consented.

"The man who'd sued the Crown consented, and I asked the registrar of the court to clear it with the judge. The registrar retired behind the scenes and shortly afterward came back to say that it was okay. I later learned that he didn't speak to the judge, who was asleep, but took it on his own to give approval.

"When I was partly through my argument, the judge roused himself and said, 'You haven't mentioned the witness Egan. It's a good thing, too, because that witness did not impress me at all.' "

Oh, the frustrations of advocacy! Ottawa lawyer Kenneth C. Binks, Q.C., likes to tell of the time he heard one of the top local counsel, Rowell Laishley, Q.C., argue a motion before the late Mr. Justice Aldous Aylen of the Supreme Court of Ontario. Mr. Laishley, armed to the teeth with precedents, read long excerpts from all of the law reports lined up in front of him.

"All the while," Binks says, "His Lordship's head was swivelling back and forth, back and forth, as he looked all around the room, barely listening. Mr. Laishley quoted from one law report after another, for an hour and a half. When he was finished, he stopped and sat down. All of a sudden, the judge's head stopped turning and he said, 'Yes, Mr. Laishley, what was that you were saying?' "

Sir William Mulock, who was born in 1844 and served as Chief Justice of Ontario for a zillion years, didn't retire from the bench until he was ninety-two. When he was a mere eighty-five, he turned down the office of lieutenant-governor of the province because it was only a five-year proposition. "If I take that job," he told friends, "in a few years I'll be left with nothing to do." As it turned out, Sir William was right, for he didn't shuffle off this mortal coil until 1944, when he was well into his 101st year.

Professor Graham Parker of Osgoode Hall Law School, York University, files this report on the venerable gentleman: "Ottawa had had complaints that the members of the Ontario Court of Appeal were getting a little long in the tooth. One of those members was Chief Justice Mulock, who was about 132 years old at that time.

"The Prime Minister of Canada sent his minister of justice to Toronto to gently tell the chief justice that it was time to retire. The minister of justice had an interview with Mulock. He was very diplomatic and told him that the PM was rather concerned that some of the members of the Court of Appeal were a little beyond it. Of course, the minister of justice intended to include the chief justice in that remark.

"Mulock listened carefully and then said, 'I quite agree. I have been telling them for ages, but they never listen!' "

A few years ago Chief Justice Gregory Evans of the High Court of Justice of Ontario received a questionnaire from a law student, asking him to advise "how many judges you have on your court, broken down by sex." The chief justice replied, "I don't have any judges who are broken down by sex, but I have several who are seriously endangered by alcohol."

The late Joseph W. Thompson, Q.C., practised law in Toronto for fifty-seven years, mostly in the field of automobile litigation. His former partner, Richard D. (Dick) McLean, Q.C., speaks lovingly of his mentor, calling him "one of the best civil jury lawyers Ontario has ever produced."

Born and raised in the country, near the village of Chesley, Ontario, Thompson taught school in the area before marching off to World War I. When hostilities ceased, he returned to school and studied law. A tall, good-looking man who always wore a rose in his lapel, Joe Thompson loved talking to juries – especially country juries. He talked to hundreds of them all over Ontario, and every time he did, McLean says, he played the country bumpkin. "Joe knew people," Dick adds, "and he applied his knowledge of people and country life to his folksy jury addresses."

McLean says that one day he was looking for something on Joe's desk when he spied a note recently written by a judge of the Supreme Court of Ontario. It said: "Dear Joe – One of these days I'm going to have to tell a jury that even a prominent defence counsel such as yourself could not have had his mother born in every county in this province."

Mr. Justice Willard Estey of the Supreme Court of Canada recalls that his former boss, The Right Honourable Bora Laskin, Chief Justice of Canada, once was a promising shortstop for a baseball team in Fort William, Ontario. His Lordship writes: "One day, Harry Arthurs, then dean of Osgoode Hall Law School, was in Fort William (now part of Thunder Bay) and, riding in from the airport in a taxi, he happened to drive by Laskin's Furniture Store, operated by Bora's older brother.

"The sight of the name Laskin prompted Harry Arthurs, a long-time friend of Bora's, to ask the cab driver if he happened to know Bora Laskin in his youth, to which the driver replied: 'Bora. Bora Laskin. Oh, yeah, a pretty good shortstop. I often wondered what became of him.' "

Winnipeg lawyer Graeme Haig, Q.C., likes to tell yarns about Louis Morosnick, a colourful "old-time" lawyer who practised for many years in the Manitoba capital. Morosnick was known as "Louie the Weep" because he could cry on cue and induce widespread sobbing in the jury box.

One day back in the 1950s Haig heard the first few minutes of a Morosnick jury address in a murder case, then had to leave to attend to some business of his own. When he returned a couple of hours later, he met a court attendant as he was leaving the courtroom.

"How's Louie the Weep doing?" Haig asked.

"Not bad," the attendant replied. "So far, he's had the fellow acquitted twice and convicted three times."

Toronto lawyer David A. Cuthbertson tells of a friend who was selected for a jury panel in Peel County, Ontario. While waiting to be called, the man fell into conversation with one of the court attendants. Knowing that Pearson International Airport was within the court's jurisdiction, he expected there'd be a great many immigration or smuggling cases.

"What type of case is most commonly heard in this court?" he asked the attendant.

"We get a lot of freedom fighters," the man replied.

"That sounds intriguing," the prospective juror remarked. "What are they fighting for?"

"Divorces," came the reply.

What's in a name? W. Andrew LeMesurier, a lawyer in Saint John, New Brunswick, tells us that in that city in December 1985, a man named Outhouse was sentenced to thirty days in jail for stealing three boxes of Ex-lax.

Toronto lawyer Garry K. Braund, Q.C., was present one morning when the judge opened court by asking crisply, "Any adjournments?"

A man at the back of the courtroom jumped to his feet and announced, "*I'm* a German!"

Lawyer Hal Lendon of Owen Sound, Ontario, reports that in early 1987 two men went to trial for breaking into an Ottawa clothing store and making off with a quantity of men's duds. They pleaded not guilty to the charges.

The store clerk took a good look at one of the men in the dock, then announced: "Your Honour, that man's wearing my jacket!"

"Are you sure?" asked the judge.

"Yes, that's my jacket!"

The Crown Attorney removed the coat from the accused and handed it to the clerk.

"See?" said the clerk. "It's even got my name in it!"

Defence counsel conferred quickly with his clients and declared that they were switching their pleas to guilty.

Toronto criminal lawyer William G. Murphy recalls a case in the 1950s in which a man was charged with stealing another man's coat. The complainant took the stand and described his coat in minute detail. The Crown Attorney showed him Exhibit A – a man's coat – and when he'd examined it the witness confirmed that, yes, this was definitely his coat.

"Ask him to try it on," the accused whispered to his lawyer, Tom Delaney.

"We can't do that," Delaney whispered back. "It'll be game over, for sure!"

"Tell him to try it on," the accused insisted.

"Try it on," Delaney said, handing the coat to the witness.

The man did as instructed. The sleeves were too short and the coat wouldn't button.

It was game over, all right – for the *Crown*.

"The accused is acquitted," the judge declared.

Out on the street, Delaney asked his client, "What ever possessed you to insist that he try on the coat?"

"I figured I was going to be arrested," the man replied, "so I had the coat altered."

Provincial Court Judge Patrick H. Curran of Halifax tells of a case that's become legendary in Nova Scotia legal circles. A man on trial for a minor offence had complained about rough treatment at the hands of the police. His main beef was that an officer had placed handcuffs too tightly on his wrists.

While a policeman was on the stand, the prosecutor decided to demonstrate the use of handcuffs.

"Do you have your 'cuffs with you?" he asked the officer.

"Yes, but –"

"Good. Now put them on me."

"Do I *have* to?"

"Yes. Do as I say."

"Well, all right, but –"

"Officer, put the 'cuffs on my wrists!"

Reluctantly, the man did as he was told.

"The prosecutor then proceeded to struggle mightily in the 'cuffs, demonstrating for all to see the painful effects of such a struggle," Judge Curran writes. "His hands turned red and then purple.

"Satisfied that his demonstration had proved the accused was the author of his own misfortune, the prosecutor asked the officer to re-move the 'cuffs. The officer replied, 'I can't.'

" 'What do you mean, you can't?' the prosecutor asked angrily. 'Take them off!'

" 'I can't,' the officer repeated, with a sheepish smile. 'I left my key back at the detachment.' "

Mr. Justice McLeod A. Craig of the Supreme Court of Ontario has a grip-ping story about his colleague, Madam Justice Mabel Van Camp.

Her Ladyship was scheduled to preside at a sitting of the court in Chatham. Since she didn't drive, she'd arranged to fly to Windsor, where she'd be met by the sheriff and driven forty miles east to Chatham in time for the opening of court.

The sheriff wasn't at the Windsor airport. Madam Justice Van Camp waited and waited, but he still didn't show. Her Ladyship took a train to Chatham, where she waited and waited again. On the platform, she saw a well-dressed man in a bowler hat.

"Excuse me," she said, "are you the sheriff?"

"Lady, you've been watching too many westerns," the man replied, walking away.

Madam Justice Van Camp took a taxi to the courthouse. At the court office, no one noticed her because they were all talking excitedly on the phone. She rapped on the counter for attention.

One of the workers looked up and said, "We can't talk to you now. We've lost the bloody judge!"

Judge Walder G. W. White of the Provincial Court of Alberta tells a touch-ing tale about the late Magistrate F. W. Barclay of Edmonton: "For quite some time, Magistrate Barclay had the habit on most Friday afternoons of adjourning court for fifteen minutes. Everyone in court was glad for the break, and they'd all go out into the hall and light up a cigarette. No sooner were their cigarettes lit than word would get around that Magis-trate Barclay was back in court. They would all quickly butt their ciga-rettes and return to court for the rest of the afternoon.

"Why he did this no one could figure out, until one Friday, as he walked down a public corridor, he turned to a down-and-out character who regularly sat in the back of the courtroom (he had nowhere else to go) and was heard by one of the clerks to ask if he'd gotten enough butts for the next week.

"Apparently Magistrate Barclay had taken a liking to the old fellow and knew that he was scrounging butts in the courthouse. By cutting the adjournment short he was ensuring a good supply of extra-long butts."

District Court Judge Ray Stortini of Sault Ste. Marie, Ontario, writes: "In March 1967 the Ontario Legal Aid Plan went into effect. One of the features was duty counsel for all provincial criminal courts. As area director, I decided to handle the first week or so to iron out any 'bugs' in the system. Thereafter I would train other counsel, and so on.

"At 9:00 A.M. on the first morning of the new plan, I attended at the old police station adjacent to the Sault Ste. Marie courthouse. I asked the duty sergeant if there were any persons in custody in the police cells. He told me there was a drunk in the bullpen downstairs.

"I went down and saw a man lying on the cot in the cell. I rattled the bars and asked, 'Do you want legal aid?' No answer. I hollered again, 'Do you want legal aid?'

"The not-fully-recovered man stirred and grunted, 'No lemonade! COF-FEE, COFFEE!' "

In 1985 Robert B. McGee, Q.C., and fellow lawyer Al Mintz were sitting in a Toronto courtroom, waiting for their cases to be called, when they heard a "Peeping Tom" case involving a man who for many years had been a plumber for a department store.

Evidence disclosed that the man had bored a hole into a women's washroom while doing some plumbing repairs, and for *twenty years* he'd spent his lunch hours watching women answer various calls of nature.

The facts were admitted, and the accused's lawyer made a technical argument that failed. The man was convicted and placed on probation.

McGee and Mintz had noticed two ladies, seventy-ish in age, sitting in the courtroom and taking a great deal of interest in the proceedings. Later, at lunch, the lawyers saw the same two women in a nearby restaurant. "They approached us," McGee writes, "and asked us to explain the judge's decision and sentence. We did.

"They told us they were two of the women the man had been watching through the peephole.

"I asked them why they had bothered with the embarrassment of coming to court, as all the facts were admitted.

"One of the old girls replied, 'He's been watching our ass for twenty years, now we're watching his!' "

Judge Dwayne Wade Rowe of the Territorial Court of the Yukon files this report on his former law partner, Chris Evans, Q.C., of Calgary:

"For a mercifully brief time early in his career, Chris Evans was the Crown Prosecutor in Medicine Hat. One day he received a report from a detective concerning a rape case. The detective had examined the woman's underclothing and found evidence of spermatozoa. But he couldn't spell the word. He wrote 'spermetta' and then crossed it out. Then he wrote something like 'spacamata' and crossed that out too. Then he wrote 'spimalgina' or some such thing, and put a heavy line through that word as well. Finally, in obvious frustration, the fellow wrote, in huge letters, 'GREAT GOBS OF WHITE STUFF.'

"James D. Horsman, long-time cabinet minister from Medicine Hat and now Attorney General of Alberta, was defence counsel in the case. Chris Evans provided Jim with a photocopy of the detective's report. In the ensuing years, every time Evans and Horsman meet up with each other, whether in an airport or in a restaurant or at a Law Society meeting, or even in the company of people like Peter Lougheed, one of them will say 'spermetta' and the other will say 'spacalicamata' or whatever other word springs to mind, and they'll go on like this until they end up saying, in unison, 'GREAT GOBS OF WHITE STUFF.' "

Oliver H. Smith, Q.C., was a big, friendly man who practised law for over forty years in Midland, Ontario. One day near the end of his career, in 1959, Oliver was sitting at the roll-top desk in his rustic office, regaling the new lawyer in town, Frederick E. Horton, with stories of some of his most colourful trials. He interrupted his narration, every now and then, to unleash a stream of tobacco juice in the general direction of a nearby spitoon. Several of these handy receptacles had been placed at strategic locations around the premises, and young Mr. Horton couldn't help noting that the floors in this establishment were very slippery indeed.

In an earlier time, Oliver recalled, he'd been consulted by a woman who was mighty concerned about her husband. The man of the house, it appeared, had been having a torrid affair with the family sow. His missus had plenty of evidence, and she instructed Oliver Smith to bring an action for divorce, based on bestiality.

The woman proved her case at trial. In six months she'd be eligible to apply for a judgment absolute, and the marriage would then be history.

"Now I'm going to show you a letter I got from her four months later," Smith told Frederick E. Horton, Q.C., who practises these days in Barrie, Ontario.

The letter was short and snappy, and Horton read it several times. That's why he remembers it, word for word. This is what it said:

P.S.

How time flies when you're having fun! It seems like only yesterday I was mooching stories for this volume, and now I'm at it again. Readers keep clamouring for funny legal anecdotes. They keep encouraging me to dig up more. It appears they can't get enough.

Still More Court Jesters is taking shape, but it needs lots of tender, loving care – from you, the readers – before it can make its debut.

Come on, now, folks, let's have those true, humorous legal tales – the sooner the better, the more the merrier. Just slide 'em to me, by letter or tape, at the address shown below.

As before, the names of contributors will be gratefully recorded for posterity. This is the chance you've been waiting for – your golden opportunity to crack into big-time showbiz. Don't blow it!

PETER V. MacDONALD, Q.C.
302-10th Street
Hanover, Ontario
N4N 1P3

Contributors

Bruce Affleck, Q.C. – Oshawa, Ont.
John S. Alexander, Q.C. – Barrie, Ont.
William Andrews, Q.C. – Toronto, Ont.
Denis Archambault – Prince George, B.C.
Hon. John Arnup – Toronto, Ont.
Robert Ash, Q.C. – Toronto, Ont.
Donald J. Avison – Ottawa, Ont.
Earl A. Bamford – Nanaimo, B.C.
John P. Barry, Q.C. – Saint John, N.B.
Paul Bates – Islington, Ont.
Judge Paul R. Belanger – Ottawa, Ont.
David P. Bellwood – Vancouver, B.C.
Daniel R. Bereskin, Q.C. – Toronto, Ont.
Mr. Justice Ronald L. Berger – Edmonton, Alta.
Mr. Justice Anthime Bergeron – Montreal, Que.
S. Tupper Bigelow, Q.C. – Toronto, Ont.
Kenneth C. Binks, Q.C. – Ottawa, Ont.
Thomas J. Bishop – Campbell River, B.C.
C. J. W. Biss – Saskatoon, Sask.
Alexander J. Black – Edmonton, Alta.
Chief Judge G. L. Bladon – Whitehorse, Y.T.
Robert V. Blakely – Vernon, B.C.
Mr. Justice Jules Blanchet – Montreal, Que.
L. M. Blond – Vancouver, B.C.
Gordon J. Z. Bobesich – Sudbury, Ont.
Mr Justice Jean-Guy Boilard – Montreal, Que.
Roland Boone – Whitehorse, Y.T.
Eric Bowie, Q.C. – Ottawa, Ont.
John E. Bradley – Fort Frances, Ont.
Garry K. Braund, Q.C. – Toronto, Ont.
Peter Breen – Toronto, Ont.
W. P. Brideaux – Ottawa, Ont.
David Brisbin – Emerson, Man.
David Brown – Ottawa, Ont.
Kingsley Brown – Antigonish, N.S.

Harry Bruce – Halifax, N.S.
Patricia L. Buchholz – Annapolis Royal, N.S.
Lee A. Burgess – Ottawa, Ont.
George C. Butterill – Toronto, Ont.
William E. Byers, Q.C. – Whitehorse, Y.T.
Norman E. Byrne, Q.C. – Hamilton, Ont.
Judge Felix A. Cacchione – Halifax, N.S.
Richard Cairns – Cranbrook, B.C.
W. Kenneth Campbell – Ottawa, Ont.
William M. Carlyle – Vancouver, B.C.
Kevin D. Carroll, Q.C. – Barrie, Ont.
William J. Carroll – Ottawa, Ont.
Mr. Justice Douglas H. Carruthers – Toronto, Ont.
Prof. Roger Carter – Saskatoon, Sask.
Leslie F. Cashman – Nanaimo, B.C.
James B. Chadwick, Q.C. – Ottawa, Ont.
Rod J. Chisholm, Q.C. – Antigonish, N.S.
William Church, Q.C. – Orangeville, Ont.
Judge James A. Clare – Barrie, Ont.
Jennifer Clark – Kitchener, Ont.
Chief Justice Lorne O. Clarke – Halifax, N.S.
Richard N. Clarke, Q.C. – Orillia, Ont.
Al Clouston – St. John's, Nfld.
David P. Cole – Toronto, Ont.
Michael G. Coleman – Duncan, B.C.
Judge R. N. Conroy – Saskatoon, Sask.
G. B. Cooke – Renfrew, Ont.
Donald M. Cooper – Yellowknife, N.W.T.
Hon. Gordon Cooper – Halifax, N.S.
William H. Corbett – Ottawa, Ont.
Rod A. Cormack, Q.C. – Toronto, Ont.
Gerard Coulombe – Montreal, Que.
R. P. K. Cousland – Toronto, Ont.
Alan L. Cox – Victoria, B.C.
A. William Cox, Q.C. – Halifax, N.S.
Mr. Justice McLeod A. Craig – Toronto, Ont.
J. Harley Crawford, Q.C. – Wingham, Ont.
Mr. Justice Paul S. Creaghan – Newcastle, N.B.
Judge Kenneth L. Crockett – Edmonton, Alta.
Chesley Crosbie – St. John's, Nfld.

Robert M. Crosby – Glace Bay, N.S.
Paul J. Crowe – Toronto, Ont.
Judge Patrick H. Curran – Halifax, N.S.
Grant M. Currie – Saskatoon, Sask.
George F. Curtis, Q.C. – Vancouver, B.C.
Ray Cuthbert – Toronto, Ont.
David A. Cuthbertson – Toronto, Ont.
H. H. Dahlem, Q.C. – Saskatoon, Sask.
Judge Timothy T. Daley – Halifax, N.S.
Murray Davidson – Ottawa, Ont.
Clyde R. Davis – Golden, B.C.
David C. Day, Q.C. – St. John's, Nfld.
Wilfred A. Day – Port Hope, Ont.
Robert Del Frate – Sudbury, Ont.
Maria De Michele – Montreal, Que.
Robert Densmore – Calgary, Alta.
Paul Derro – Sudbury, Ont.
Philippe Desjardins – Ottawa, Ont.
John H. Dickey, Q.C. – Halifax, N.S.
Christine Dickson – Wingham, Ont.
D. J. Dickson – London, Ont.
Henry J. Dietrich – Halifax, N.S.
Judge Robert B. Dnieper – Toronto, Ont.
Senator Richard A. Donahoe, Q.C. – Halifax, N.S.
Terence R. B. Donahoe, Q.C. – Halifax, N.S.
Alan W. Donaldson – Kelowna, B.C.
Mr. Justice Jacques Ducros – Montreal, Que.
Bob Duncanson – Kitchener, Ont.
John G. Dunlap, Q.C. – Ottawa, Ont.
W. Dale Dunlop – Halifax, N.S.
Gerald A. Dust – Orleans, Ont.
L. Murray Eades – Mississauga, Ont.
Rev. George Earle – St. John's, Nfld.
Randell J. Earle – St. John's, Nfld.
Keith E. Eaton, Q.C. – Chester Basin, N.S.
Thomas G. Edmondstone – Renfrew, Ont.
William M. Elliott, Q.C. – Regina, Sask.
Mr. Justice Willard Estey – Ottawa, Ont.
Mr. Justice Gregory Evans – Toronto, Ont.
Robert F. Evans – Bradford, Ont.

R. J. Falkins – Sault Ste. Marie, Ont.
Peter Fallis – Durham, Ont.
Brian R. Farmer – Walkerton, Ont.
Francis X. Fay, Q.C. – Toronto, Ont.
Mr. Justice Joseph Bernard Feehan – Edmonton, Alta.
Melanie Fendley – London, Ont.
Dan S. Ferguson – Toronto, Ont.
Roderic G. Ferguson, Q.C. – Midland, Ont.
Alan D. Fielding – Camrose, Alta.
John L. Fingarson – Calgary, Alta.
Charles C. Finley – Toronto, Ont.
Judge F. Stewart Fisher – Etobicoke, Ont.
James L. Floyd – Penticton, B.C.
Winston Fogarty – Ottawa, Ont.
Peter B. Forbes, Q.C. – Brantford, Ont.
Judge M. P. Forestell – Cayuga, Ont.
Jennifer M. Foy – Calgary, Alta.
Duncan Fraser, Q.C. – Brockville, Ont.
J. W. Fraser – Pembroke, Ont.
Hon. Samuel Freedman – Winnipeg, Man.
Ronald J. Fromstein – Ajax, Ont.
Frank A. Gabriel – Toronto, Ont.
Hon. G. A. Gale – Toronto, Ont.
Michael J. Galligan, Q.C. – Almonte, Ont.
Robert W. Garcia – Hanover, Ont.
D. E. Gauley, Q.C. – Saskatoon, Sask.
Jacques Gauthier – St. Joseph, N.B.
Debbie George – Sydney, N.S.
Rod Germaine – Vancouver, B.C.
John D. Gibson – Toronto, Ont.
J. Robert Gibson – Toronto, Ont.
Mary Louise Gilman – Hanover, Mass.
C. Stephen Glithero – Kitchener, Ont.
Ashley R. Gnys – Niagara Falls, Ont.
G. W. Goetz, Q.C. – Guelph, Ont.
Arnell Goldberg, Q.C. – Ottawa, Ont.
Chief Justice Noel Goodridge – St. John's, Nfld.
Jack Gordon – Hanover, Ont.
Stephen T. Goudge, Q.C. – Toronto, Ont.
Cal Graham – Toronto, Ont.

Fred Graham – Barrie, Ont.
Lawrence Graham – Dartmouth, N.S.
Margaret Graham – Dartmouth, N.S.
Brian L. Graves – Comox, B.C.
L. C. Green – Edmonton, Alta.
William T. Green, Q.C. – Ottawa, Ont.
James J. Greene, Q.C. – St. John's, Nfld.
Edward L. Greenspan, Q.C. – Toronto, Ont.
Judge William Gunn – Halifax, N.S.
Chief Judge Harold Gyles – Winnipeg, Man.
Mr. Justice William J. Haddad – Edmonton, Alta.
Douglas G. Haig, Q.C. – Midland, Ont.
Graeme Haig, Q.C. – Winnipeg, Man.
David A. Hain – Brockville, Ont.
Martin Haley – Halifax, N.S.
Judge Robert Halifax – Whitehorse, Y.T.
Mr. Justice Doane Hallett – Halifax, N.S.
Mr. Justice Raymond Halley – St. John's, Nfld.
Mr. Justice John R. Hannan – Montreal, Que.
Mr. Justice A. Milton Harradence – Calgary, Alta.
Judge Sydney M. Harris – Toronto, Ont.
David Hay – Owen Sound, Ont.
R. L. Hendrie – Toronto, Ont.
T. Michael Hennessy – Sudbury, Ont.
William Hesler – Montreal, Que.
Linda M. Heyder – Burk's Falls, Ont.
Robert H. Hickman – Toronto, Ont.
Chief Justice Alexander Hickman – St. John's, Nfld.
Tim J. Hilborn – Cambridge, Ont.
Robert L. Holden – Toronto, Ont.
George R. Holland – Kelowna, B.C.
John D. Hope – Nanaimo, B.C.
Frederick E. Horton, Q.C. – Barrie, Ont.
Judge Jacie C. Horwitz – Ottawa, Ont.
George R. Houlding, Q.C. – Brantford, Ont.
Judge Edward J. Houston – Ottawa, Ont.
Kenneth G. Houston, Q.C. – Winnipeg, Man.
Robert E. Houston, Q.C. – Ottawa, Ont.
Robert B. Howe – Barry's Bay, Ont.
F. A. Huckabone, Q.C. – Pembroke, Ont.

Jan Hudson – Vancouver, B.C.
Jack Hughes – Toronto, Ont.
Irene Hussey – Cambridge, Ont.
P. A. Insley – Victoria, B.C.
Tom Irvine – Kingston, Ont.
Julius Isaac, Q.C. – Ottawa, Ont.
Angelika Jamal – Vancouver, B.C.
R. R. Jeffels – B.C.
M. Robert Jette – Saint John, N.B.
Dean Jobb – Halifax, N.S.
Doreen Johnson – Edmonton, Alta.
Eileen Johnson – Markham, Ont.
Gerald R. Johnson – Walkerton, Ont.
Robert T. C. Johnston – Victoria, B.C.
William D. Johnston – Peterborough, Ont.
Mr. Justice Fred Kaufman – Montreal, Que.
Roydon J. Kealey, Q.C. – Ottawa, Ont.
John D. Keast – Sudbury, Ont.
Karla Keddy – Halifax, N.S.
Lisa Keller – Winnipeg, Man.
Janet C. Kelly – Manotick, Ont.
Mr. Justice William Kelly – Halifax, N.S.
Andrew Kemp – Prince George, B.C.
Edward B. Kendall – Midland, Ont.
Judge Joseph P. Kennedy – Bridgewater, N.S.
Donald A. Kerr, Q.C. – Halifax, N.S.
Digby R. Kier – Vancouver, B.C.
Harvey J. Kirsh – Toronto, Ont.
Bruce H. Knapp – Peterborough, Ont.
Maria Kosior – Edmonton, Alta.
Jerry D. Kovacs – Windsor, Ont.
Mr. Justice Horace Krever – Toronto, Ont.
Judge R.J. Kucey – Saskatoon, Sask.
Henry A. Kurki – Mar, Ont.
Gordon J. Kuski, Q.C. – Regina, Sask.
Alfred M. Kwinter – Toronto, Ont.
R.W. Lalande – Sudbury, Ont.
C. Maxwell Lane – St. John's, Nfld.
Robert J. Lane – Shellbrook, Sask.
Judge Douglas Latimer – Milton, Ont.

David G. Lawrence – Toronto, Ont.
R. Bruce Leach – Pembroke, Ont.
Louise LeBlanc – Ottawa, Ont.
Ronald J. LeBlanc – Moncton, N.B.
W. Merrill Leckie – Vancouver, B.C.
Gerald J. Lecovin – Vancouver, B.C.
Thomas M. Ledebur – Regina, Sask.
S. G. Leggett, Q.C. – North York, Ont.
W. Andrew LeMesurier – Saint John, N.B.
Hal Lendon – Owen Sound, Ont.
Mr. Justice Rodman E. Logan – Saint John, N.B.
Michael Lomer – Toronto, Ont.
Bernard Loomis – Vernon, B.C.
S. D. Loukidelis – Sudbury, Ont.
David L. Lovell – Owen Sound, Ont.
Richard B. Low – Calgary, Alta.
Dorothy G. Lynch – Winnipeg, Man.
Daniel Lyon – Toronto, Ont.
Patrick MacAdam – Ottawa, Ont.
Alan MacDonald – Calgary, Alta.
Mr. Justice Angus L. Macdonald – Halifax, N.S.
Paul MacDonald – St. John's, Nfld.
Judge Ronald Angus MacDonald – Antigonish, N.S.
Rosemary MacDonald – Calgary, Alta.
Douglas MacEachern – Edmonton, Alta.
William MacEachern – Ottawa, Ont.
Judge H. R. MacEwan – New Glasgow, N.S.
Charles W. MacIntosh, Q.C. – Halifax, N.S.
George K. MacIntosh – Vancouver, B.C.
Ronald F. MacIsaac – Victoria, B.C.
Laurie MacKay – Fort Saskatchewan, Alta.
Prof. Robert S. Mackay – London, Ont.
Patric Mackesy – Hamilton, Ont.
Wayne Mackie – Vancouver, B.C.
Mr. Justice Douglas B. MacKinnon – Vancouver, B.C.
Mr. Justice L. D. MacLean – Lethbridge, Alta.
Frank Maczko, Q.C. – Vancouver, B.C.
Ted J. Madison – London, Ont.
Mr. Justice John H. Maher – Saskatoon, Sask.
Mr. Justice Patrick M. Mahoney – Ottawa, Ont.

David C. Marriott – Leduc, Alta.
Mr. Justice Ernest A. Marshall – Edmonton, Alta.
Ruth J. Masters – Courtenay, B.C.
Herbert L. Matthews – Victoria, B.C.
Weldon C. Matthews – Halifax, N.S.
Anthony J. Maytum – Vancouver, B.C.
Al McCann – Edmonton, Alta.
Ed McCarroll – Toronto, Ont.
Judge Robert J. McCleave – Halifax, N.S.
Mr. Justice John W. McClung – Edmonton, Alta.
Eric D. McCooeye – Sault Ste. Marie, Ont.
David O. McCray – Walkerton, Ont.
Donald F. McCrimmon – Medicine Hat, Alta.
Chief Justice Allan McEachern – Vancouver, B.C.
Robert B. McGee, Q.C. – Toronto, Ont.
Gail McGilvray – London, Ont.
Daniel H. McGuire – Ottawa, Ont.
Jon M. McGuire – Winnipeg, Man.
Anne McIntyre – Fenelon Falls, Ont.
Robert D. McIntyre – Brampton, Ont.
Judge J. Ian McKay – Walkerton, Ont.
Colin D. McKinnon, Q.C. – Ottawa, Ont.
Richard D. McLean, Q.C. – Toronto, Ont.
Judge R. F. McLellan – Truro, N.S.
Grant McLennan, Q.C. – Perth, Ont.
Heather McLeran – Winnipeg, Man.
Mr. Justice Nicholson D. McRae – Toronto, Ont.
Mr. Justice Pierre Michaud – Montreal, Que.
Gordon Michener, Q.C. – Orillia, Ont.
Maria Mihailovich – Hamilton, Ont.
Mr. Justice Michel A. Monnin – Winnipeg, Man.
Daniel W. Monteith – Newmarket, Ont.
Michelle Monteyne – Dorchester, Ont.
Carla Moors – Thunder Bay, Ont.
Rene Monty – Key West, Fla.
Tom Moran – Toronto, Ont.
J. Rhys Morgan, Q.C. – Napanee, Ont.
S. Wayne Morris – Toronto, Ont.
Matti E. Mottonen – Sudbury, Ont.
David Muise – Sydney, N.S.

John Pius Mulcahy – St. John's, Nfld.
Stephen J. Mulhall – Vancouver, B.C.
Gregory M. Mulligan – Orillia, Ont.
Daniel J. Murphy, Q.C. – Goderich, Ont.
Greg Murphy – Bridgewater, N.S.
William G. Murphy – Toronto, Ont.
Mr. Justice George L. Murray – Vancouver, B.C.
Chief Justice N. T. Nemetz – Vancouver, B.C.
E. Peter Newcombe, Q.C. – Ottawa, Ont.
Judge Paul Niedermayer – Dartmouth, N.S.
Mr. Justice Nathaniel S. Noel – St. John's, Nfld.
Mr. Justice John A. Nolan – Montreal, Que.
W. Wayne Norris – Clearbrook, B.C.
Judge J. B. J. Nutting – Saskatoon, Sask.
Gerry O'Brien – St. John's, Nfld.
Fergus J. O'Connor – Kingston, Ont.
Michael O'Driscoll – Toronto, Ont.
H. A. D. Oliver, Q.C. – Vancouver, B.C.
Hugh O'Neill, Q.C. – St. John's, Nfld.
Judge Seamus B. O'Regan – Happy Valley–Goose Bay, Nfld.
Tom O'Reilly, Q.C. – St. John's, Nfld.
Frank P. Oster – Toronto, Ont.
Russell Otter, Q.C. – Toronto, Ont.
Robert A. Otto – Hamilton, Ont.
Jean N. Ouellette – Sutton, Que.
Mr. Justice George R. Owen – Montreal, Que.
Mr. Justice Leonard L. Pace – Halifax, N.S.
D. G. Pahl – Thunder Bay, Ont.
Chief Judge Ian Palmeter – Halifax, N.S.
J. Jay Park – Calgary, Alta.
Glenn G. Parker – Toronto, Ont.
Prof. Graham Parker – Downsview, Ont.
Ron Paskar – Mississauga, Ont.
Alex K. Paterson, Q.C. – Montreal, Que.
J. Patrick Peacock, Q.C. – Calgary, Alta.
Peter Pegg – Wiarton, Ont.
Judge C. Emerson Perkins – Chatham, Ont.
Hub Phelan – St. Catharines, Ont.
Joel E. Pink, Q.C. – Halifax, N.S.
Doug H. Player – Boca Raton, Fla.

William R. Poole, Q.C. – London, Ont.
Mr. Justice Joseph Potts – Toronto, Ont.
Richard W. Pound – Montreal, Que.
John R. Power, Q.C. – Ottawa, Ont.
Prof. Ronald R. Price, Q.C. – Kingston, Ont.
Robert M. Prince – Yarmouth, N.S.
Brian Purdy, Q.C. – Vancouver, B.C.
Mr. Justice Stuart S. Purvis – Edmonton, Alta.
N. J. Pustina, Q.C. – Thunder Bay, Ont.
Kenneth A. Rae, Q.C. – Owen Sound, Ont.
David Rampersad, Q.C. – Winnipeg, Man.
Judge G. Hughes Randall – Halifax, N.S.
Bert Raphael, Q.C. – Toronto, Ont.
Richard A. Reimer – Petawawa, Ont.
William L. Riley – Ottawa, Ont.
Frederick L. Ringham – Vancouver, B.C.
David Roberts, Q.C. – West Vancouver, B.C.
James T. Robson – Kitchener, Ont.
Arthur W. MacLeod Rogers, Q.C. – Victoria, B.C.
John Rorke – St. John's, Nfld.
C. M. Rosenblum, Q.C. – Sydney, N.S.
Alan M. Ross – Vancouver, B.C.
Kent A. Rowan – Edmonton, Alta.
Judge Dwayne Wade Rowe – Whitehorse, Y.T.
Douglas R. Ruddell – Parksville, B.C.
Manly S. Rusen – Winnipeg, Man.
D. J. A. Rutherford, Q.C. – Ottawa, Ont.
Andrew G. Sandilands – Vancouver, B.C.
Gregory H. Scott – Camrose, Alta.
Jill E. Scrutton – London, Ont.
Judge Gordon Seabright – St. John's, Nfld.
Kathleen Sellers – Kitchener, Ont.
Manuel Shacter, Q.C. – Montreal, Que.
Mr. Justice Melvin E. Shannon – Calgary, Alta.
Norman A. Shepherd, Q.C. – Kincardine, Ont.
Tom Sheppard – Sudbury, Ont.
Vern Sherk – Kitchener, Ont.
Irvin H. Sherman, Q.C. – Scarborough, Ont.
H. H. Sherwood – Cornwall, Ont.
John Shipley – Ottawa, Ont.

Leonard M. Shore, Q.C. – Ottawa, Ont.
Robert A. L. Shour – Toronto, Ont.
Morris C. Shumiatcher, Q.C. – Regina, Sask.
Sidney B. Simons – Vancouver, B.C.
Hal C. Sisson, Q.C. – Peace River, Alta.
Corinne Skura – Edmonton, Alta.
R. G. Smethurst – Winnipeg, Man.
Gordon Smith – Orillia, Ont.
Jerome C. Smyth, Q.C. – Montreal, Que.
Susie Sparks – Calgary, Alta.
Barry A. Spiegel, Q.C. – Toronto, Ont.
Robert H. Spring – Vancouver, B.C.
Sheila Stephenson – Walkerton, Ont.
Judge Brian C. Stevenson – Calgary, Alta.
Steve Stirling – Port Alberni, B.C.
Douglas G. Stokes – Calgary, Alta.
The Hon. Arthur J. Stone – Ottawa, Ont.
Judge Ray Stortini – Sault Ste. Marie, Ont.
Hudson J. Stowe – Toronto, Ont.
Michael F. Stoyka, Q.C. – Windsor, Ont.
Maxine L. Strain – Lethbridge, Alta.
Judge Hazen Strange – Oromocto, N.B.
Pat Sullivan – Truro, N.S.
Thomas R. Swabey – Cornwall, Ont.
Elsie E. Swartz – Toronto, Ont.
Mary E. Switek – Winnipeg, Man.
Linda M. Tippett – Dartmouth, N.S.
Judge Donald G. E. Thompson – Owen Sound, Ont.
Jane Thompson – Vancouver, B.C.
Robert C. Thompson, Q.C. – Collingwood, Ont.
Carey B. Thomson – Pembroke, Ont.
Orval J. Troy, Q.C. – Ottawa, Ont.
Lynne Tsubouchi – Markham, Ont.
Mr. Justice Claude R. Vallerand – Montreal, Que.
Brian Van De Vyvere – Walkerton, Ont.
Ellen Vezina – London, Ont.
Emanuel M. Vomberg – Calgary, Alta.
Mr. Justice Allan H. Wachowich – Edmonton, Alta.
R. Bruce Waite, Q.C. – Orillia, Ont.
Humphrey E. Waldock – Vancouver, B.C.

Harvey G. Walker – North Battleford, Sask.
Reagan Walker – Edmonton, Alta.
R. Brian Wallace – Vancouver, B.C.
H. Graham Walsh, Q.C. – Pembroke, Ont.
Donald J. Warner, Q.C. – Lindsay, Ont.
D. Reilly Watson, Q.C. – Ottawa, Ont.
Mary Weaver – Sudbury, Ont.
Judge Norris Weisman – Toronto, Ont.
Mr. Justice Robert Wells – St. John's, Nfld.
Judge Walder G. W. White – Edmonton, Alta.
Ivan G. Whitehall, Q.C. – Ottawa, Ont.
Mitchell Wine – Toronto, Ont.
S. E. Wolfson – Willowdale, Ont.
Morden L. Wolsey – Medicine Hat, Alta.
Harry E. Wrathall, Q.C. – Halifax, N.S.
Judge E. F. Wren – Toronto, Ontario
John R. Wrigley – Ottawa, Ont.
Ken Young – Ottawa, Ont.
Rose Yuke – Walkerton, Ont.
Daphne Zander – Pembroke, Ont.
Judge Robert E. Zelinski – Owen Sound, Ont.
Michael Zigayer – Ottawa, Ont.
Milton W. Zwicker – Orillia, Ont.